D0408468

e-Strategy
PURE & SIMPLE

Connecting Your Internet Strategy to Your Business Strategy

MICHEL ROBERT
BERNARD RACINE

McGraw-Hill

New York San Francisco Washington, D.C. Auckland Bogotá
Caracas Lisbon London Madrid Mexico City Milan
Montreal New Delhi San Juan Singapore
Sidney Tokyo Toronto

McGraw-Hill

A Division of The ***McGraw-Hill*** *Companies*

1 2 3 4 5 6 7 8 9 0 DOC/DOC 0 9 8 7 6 5 4 3 2 1 0

ISBN 0-07-137178-8

The sponsoring editor for this book was Richard Narramore, the editing supervisor was Maureen B. Walker, and the production supervisor was Charles Annis. It was set in Minion by Binghamton Valley Composition.

Printed and bound by R. R. Donnelley & Sons Company.

McGraw-Hill books are available at special quantity discounts to use as premiums and sales promotions, or for use in corporate training programs. For more information, please write to the Director of Special Sales, Professional Publishing, McGraw-Hill, Two Penn Plaza, New York, NY 10121-2298. Or contact your local bookstore.

This book is printed on recycled, acid-free paper containing a minimum of 50% recycled, de-inked fiber.

Contents

Preface

"I just approved a $10 million dollar Internet project and I have absolutely no idea of what it was all about," said one of our CEO clients to us a few weeks ago. Unfortunately, this is a sentiment shared by many CEOs we have encountered in the last two to three years.

They are approving large sums of money on Internet and IT projects without a clue of what they are getting. The reason is simple. These CEOs are baffled by the sudden emergence of a new variable in their universe, a variable called the Internet. And they are baffled because they simply don't understand the Internet and its implications on their business. When one doesn't understand something, one's decision-making power is paralyzed, which is what is happening to many CEOs.

As a result, they place their fate in the hands of so-called Internet Expert Consultants to develop an Internet Plan for them. This is akin to making the plumber the architect for your new house. You'll end up with a lot of pipes! In business, you'll end up with a lot of unnecessary hardware and software and possibly with an Internet plan that does not support the business strategy of the enterprise.

Our premise is that the CEO and the Executive Team should be the architect of their own Internet strategy which is connected to, and helps deploy, the enterprise's business strategy.

This book contains concepts and a process that demystifies the Internet (in "lay" terms) which then empowers CEOs and their key executives to design their own Internet strategy and thus control their own destiny.

MICHEL ROBERT
BERNARD RACINE

e-Strategy

PURE & SIMPLE

CHAPTER

The Ultimate E-Nigma

No change represents as large a challenge to every chief executive officer (CEO) now and in the years to come as the Internet. Because of the intangibility of the Internet, it is difficult for most executives to "get their arms around it." They can't see it, they can't touch it, and they have no experience with it or anything like it. As a result, most executives have great difficulty assessing the impact the Internet will have on their businesses. It's an unknown, and unknowns can be unsettling. There are very good reasons for this malaise.

THE NEW ECONOMY

In 1999 close to 50 percent of the capital investments in this country were made for information technology, or IT, as it is referred to in the vernacular. This number is projected to increase 10 to 15 percent per year for the next several years. This represents an enormous shift in the country's resources away from the traditional investment in so-called bricks and mortar and to IT. This shift is creating what has become known as the new economy. We are swiftly becoming a "wired" economy which is moving rapidly from "bricks" to "clicks."

The cause of this increasing dependency on IT is the Internet. Here are some statistics that demonstrate the rapidly growing influence of the Internet on businesses and consumers. In the last five years, the dollar amount of transactions conducted on the Internet jumped from a negligible sum to over $1.3 trillion, and this number is projected to increase at a double-digit pace for several years. To date, 80 percent of these transactions are business-to-business (B2B) and only 20 percent are business-to-consumer (B2C). The B2C portion, however, is projected to increase significantly, as the following charts indicate.

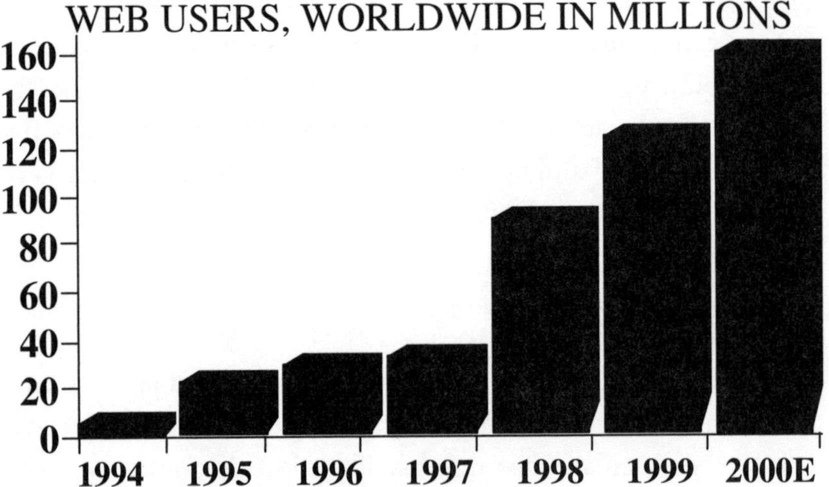

Source: International Data Corporation.

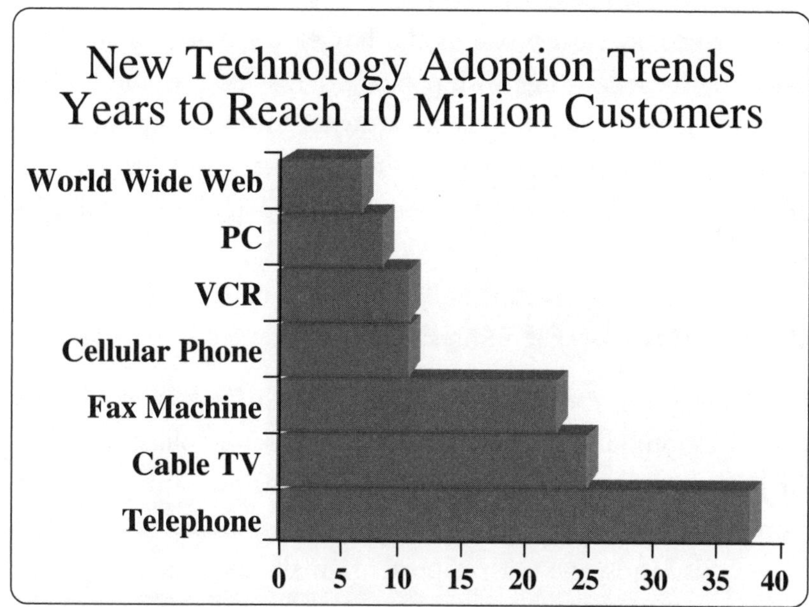

Source: International Data Corporation.

LESSONS FROM THE PAST

Let's go back in time to 1885–1886, when the first automobile was introduced. Who then could have foreseen the advent of concepts such as car insurance, autobahns, parking lots, drive-in restaurants, banks and theaters, and laser-read toll systems? The answer is simple: Probably no one. The reason? These concepts were so foreign to most people's modus operandi that they had great difficulty adapting their thinking to accommodate them. In fact, people could hardly bring themselves to give the automobile a name. At first they called it a horseless carriage because it was the first carriage that did not need to be pulled by animals or humans The best they could do was name it an automobile, which literally means "self-moving," not a terribly mesmerizing description.

Now let's examine the year 2000 and the Internet, a concept

as alien to today's executive as the horseless carriage was to the owner of the local buggy whip factory. Just as the automobile paralyzed the buggy whip factory owner from doing anything about the automobile because of its "alienness," the Internet is paralyzing today's CEO. And there are good reasons for this as well.

FROM LANDSCAPE TO SEASCAPE

Let's draw some mental pictures. Imagine a landscape with its profile of mountains, valleys, lakes, canyons, and volcanoes, all of which have been shaped by nature's forces—wind, rain, gases, and so on—in that environment. Now imagine a modern city sprouting on this landscape with a host of small, medium, and large buildings, all interconnected by a road and rail system.

A business operates in a similar manner. It also has a profile consisting of products, customers, and markets which have been shaped by all the market forces—competitive, economic, political, technological—at work in this business arena or environment. Similar to a city sprouting from a landscape, what emerges from a "business arena" is a *business model* which is put into place to deploy the business strategy of an enterprise.

Furthermore, just as the natural terrain surrounding a city puts physical constraints on that city's activities, the business "terrain" in which a company finds itself imposes constraints on that company, and those constraints obviously vary from one geographic area to another.

THE TRADITIONAL BUSINESS MODEL UNDER SIEGE

Let's draw another picture. Imagine now that the sea level rose 50 feet around the globe. Most cities on the planet would be flooded to one degree or another, and the landscape would become a seascape.

The tallest buildings would no longer be connected by *intricate* and *restrictive* road and rail systems but could be served by an *uncluttered* and *unrestricted* flat, open surface water system. Each building could be reached from any other building at any time of the day, over water.

A DRAMATIC CHANGE IN THE RULES OF PLAY

In this new environment, landscape "business practices" are now irrelevant and need to change drastically to accommodate the new seascape environment. Consider the following changes:

Speedboats can replace slow-moving trucks and trains.

Tollbooths are useless on water.

Competitors who previously could challenge you only over land now can do so in a different manner, or you could be attacked by new, unpredictable pirate ships.

Among the rules the Internet has changed are the following:

- The traditional value chain has been disrupted.
- Assets may now be liabilities.
- Brand loyalty is no longer an advantage.
- Service may no longer be a differentiator.
- A captive market has been unshackled and given numerous options.
- A customer's switching costs have been reduced significantly.
- Information is virtually "free," thus spreading like a virus and making customers much more knowledgeable.

- Pricing matches minute-to-minute market conditions.
- On-line demand drives production.

And there have been many more changes. The message is that each rule change helps make the Internet an e-nigma. This new e-business model is conceptually alien to the executives of a business rooted in the traditional business model of bricks and mortar. Furthermore, the Internet has unshackled new competitors from the constraints of the traditional business model and introduced business practices that are also alien to these executives.

Traditional relationships between suppliers, producers, distributors, and customers have been turned upside down and inside out, and the new relationships are difficult to comprehend. In other words, the sandbox is getting more and more e-nigmatic.

DENIAL OR PARANOIA

The human being's instinctive reaction to something that is unfamiliar or unknown manifests itself in one of two modes: denial or paranoia. In our view, the CEO population is currently split 50/50.

Denial is also called the ostrich reaction: Put your head in the sand and hope the event passes by. Many CEOs are doing just that. They are avoiding the Internet, hoping that it will be another fad that will pass just like the many other management fads they have seen come and go.

Paranoia characterizes a person who sees ghosts all over the place. Therefore, let's do everything and anything we can think of.

THE INTERNET MIGRATION IS INESCAPABLE

The "flood" that today is putting in jeopardy the traditional business model actually started 30 years ago with the advent of IT systems in the back office, which then migrated to the front office and now has moved into over a billion homes in only a few years. It has been well documented that a new technology becomes "institutionalized" when it reaches a critical mass of 30 million consumers. One billion users is way past the critical mass required and well beyond the inflection point where a new technology starts to accelerate its impact on society. Nothing will stop this migration, and that means that denial will not solve the e-nigma.

Paranoia is not the solution either. The reason for this is simple. The Internet *will not* intrude on every part of your current business model, but it will infringe on many nooks and crannies of that model. To anticipate where those points of impact will be, one needs to understand the *capabilities* the Internet brings and how they will be used by your competitors and how they could be used by your company.

However, before attempting to understand the Internet and its various capabilities, one needs to understand the *business strategy* of the enterprise. Unless the business strategy is clear and unambiguous, it will be difficult to determine the role the Internet should play.

TWO KEY QUESTIONS

The advent of the Internet should cause two questions to make their way to the top of a CEO's list of priorities:

1. Is our business strategy Internet-ready?
2. Do we have a coherent Internet strategy that supports our business strategy?

The future of every company today rests with an affirmative answer to both questions. Unfortunately, experience indicates that very few companies could confidently answer yes to either of those questions, much less both. In fact, experience shows that most companies would answer no to the second question and no or, at best, maybe to the first.

Not only would most companies reply that their business strategy is not ready for the Internet, many executives would question whether there is a coherent business strategy in place at all. This occurs because many organizations suffer from a malaise we call "strategic fuzziness."

CHAPTER 2

Strategic Fuzziness

For the last 20 years we have worked with over 400 companies in dozens of industries and countries, using a process we have developed and called *strategic thinking* to help those companies formulate and deploy a successful *business* strategy. The main reason CEOs have used our process is to overcome a phenomenon we call *strategic fuzziness.*

In any company, the strategy and direction of the organization should be set by the CEO with the help of the top management team. The strategy should be clear and explicit so that employees understand it and can use it as a filter or target to make intelligent and consistent decisions on behalf of the company over time. Unfortunately, in most companies the strategy is *implicit* and resides in the heads of a few people at the top, while the other members of the staff have to guess what the strategy is every time they make a decision.

Another element that adds to the difficulty of understanding the strategy of a business is that most people cannot distinguish between *strategy* and *operations.* In other words, they cannot separate *strategy* and *strategic thinking* from *operations* and *operational thinking.* Although both types of thinking go on simultaneously in every organization, they are practiced with different degrees of proficiency.

A simple method for illustrating the difference is to look at it this way: *Strategy* is *what*, and operations is *how*. In other words, strategy is the kind of thinking that involves *what we want to be*, while *operations* is the kind of thinking that indicates *how to get there*. Graphically, the difference between these concepts can be explained as it is in Figure 1.

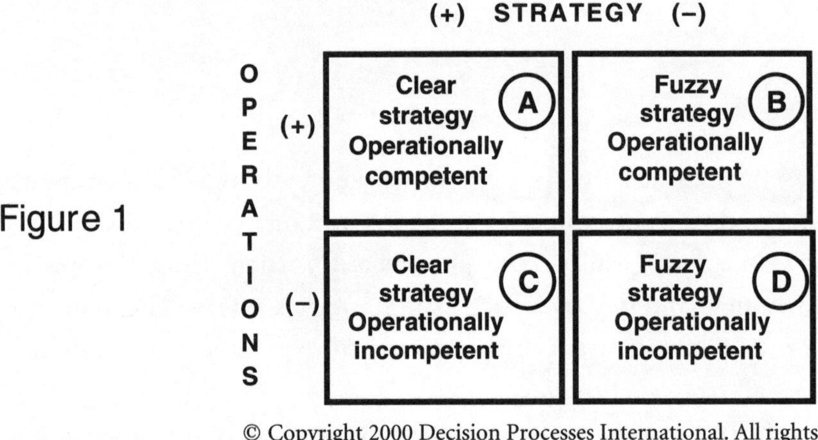

Figure 1

In quadrant A (see Figure 2), we find companies that have a well-articulated strategy that's well communicated and well understood by everyone in the organization. These companies know what they want to become. Furthermore, they are very competent operationally. They know how to get there.

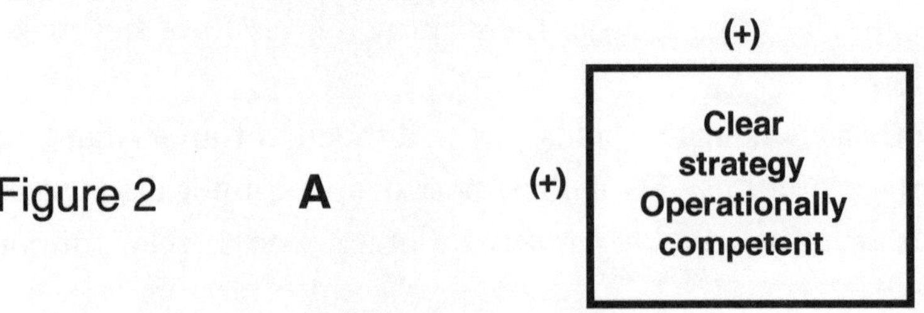

Figure 2

Examples of such companies are IBM and Lou Gerstner's formulation and deployment of his "co-centric computing" strategy. Other companies with clear strategies are Disney under Michael Eisner, Dell Computer under Michael Dell, Wal-Mart under Sam Walton and David Glass, and Home Depot under Bernie Marcus and Arthur Blank.

In quadrant B (see Figure 3), we find companies that are operationally effective but strategically deficient. Many companies that pursue a me-too strategy fall into this quadrant.

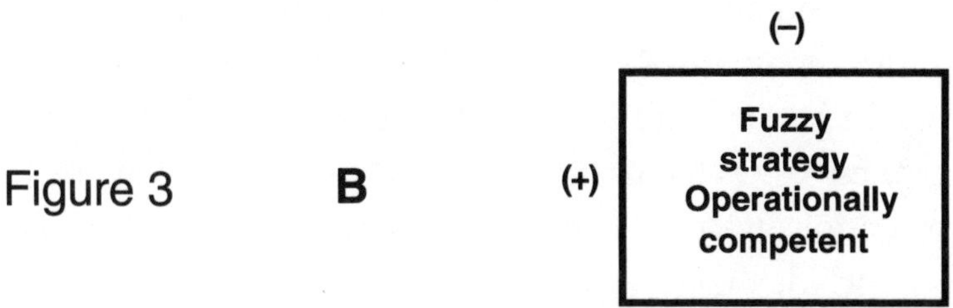

In quadrant C (see Figure 4), we find companies that have a clear strategy; their problem is making it happen operationally. A good example recently has been the personal computer (PC) industry, with its 130 to 140 competitors all trying to be the best "Wintel" clone they can be. That is a clear strategy, but unfortunately, most of them have been unable to execute well operationally, and the winners and losers change almost every day.

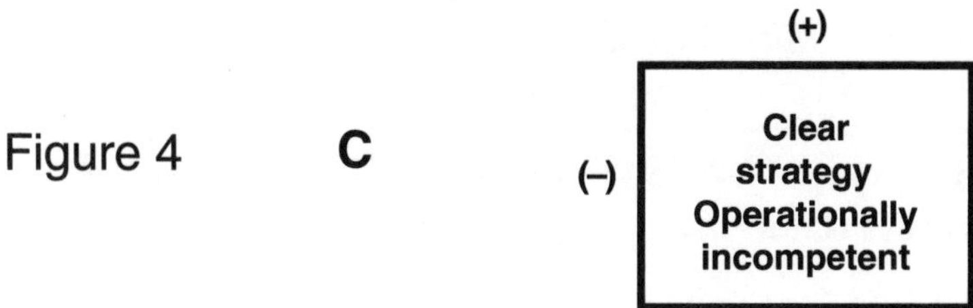

In quadrant D (see Figure 5), we find the worst of both worlds. Unfortunately, the list of examples is not very long because if you find yourself in this quadrant, you will not be around long enough to talk about it.

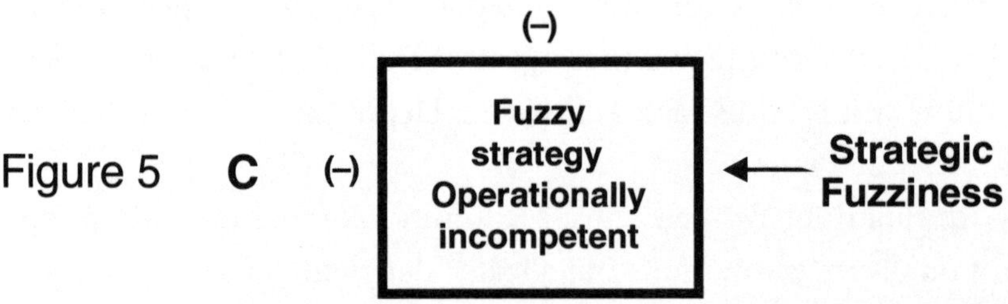

In which quadrant do you think most companies find themselves? We have posed this question to more than 3,000 CEOs all over the world, and the answer is always the same. Eighty to ninety percent of these CEOs tell us that most companies reside in quadrant B: operationally competent but strategically deficient. Many CEOs even include their own companies in this category. In other words, most executives can keep the numbers coming out right quarter after quarter, but they don't have a shared understanding of what the company will look like as a result of all that churning. We call this the Christopher Columbus School of Management:

- When he left, he did not know where he was going.
- When he got there, he did not know where he was.
- When he got back, he couldn't tell where he had been.

Do you belong to this school? To help you reply to this question, you may want to work through the following assessment.

WHAT IS THE STRATEGIC QUOTIENT OF YOUR ORGANIZATION?

The following survey is designed to have you assess the strategic IQ of your organization and determine which quadrant you fall into. The survey is designed to be answered by the CEO and the management committee. The respondents should answer the questions individually, without consulting each other, and their answers should be compared afterward. If you wish to have an objective assessment of these answers, we will gladly do it for you and do an "audit" of your strategy as well.

1. Do you have a well-articulated, clear statement of strategy?
   Yes❑10 No❑1
2. Could each member of your management team write a one or two-sentence statement of that strategy without consulting the others?
   All could ❑10 Some could ❑5 None could ❑1
3. Do you have your strategy in written form?
   Yes❑10 No❑5
4. Do you and they use this statement as a guide for the choices you make together when deciding which products, customers, and markets your company will pursue?
   Use frequently ❑10 Use sometimes ❑5 Never use ❑1
5. Do you and they use this statement as a guide to decide which products, customers, and markets your company will not pursue?
   Use frequently ❑10 Use sometimes ❑5 Never use ❑1
6. Do you use this statement as a tool to decide how resources are allocated within the company?
7. Do you use this statement as a tool to choose which opportunities your company will pursue and which ones it won't?
   Use frequently ❑10 Use sometimes ❑5 Never use ❑1
8. Have you ever sat down as a management team to try to obtain consensus about the future direction of the organization?
   Regularly 10❑ Once in a while ❑3 Never ❑1
9. Was a consensus obtained, or are there still different visions of what the organization is trying to become?
   One vision ❑10 Several visions ❑1 No vision ❑1
10. Do you have a *separate* process of strategic thinking to determine

what you want to become as opposed to *how* you will get there?
Formal, codified process ❑10 No process ❑1

Total Score ________

If all the answers are similar and each statement is identical, you are in good shape. The wider the discrepancies are in their replies compared to yours, the less clear your strategy is to them, and you may want to entertain the idea of taking your management team through the process described in the remainder of this book.

Scoring Your Strategic IQ

If you wish to get a numerical assessment of your strategic quotient, simply add up the scores next to all the questions to which you responded. The following is our assessment of your score.

Score: 100

You're perfect. There is no need for you to read the remainder of this book unless you don't know *why* you are so good.

Score: 70–99

There is some degree of ambiguity over strategy among the management team, with periodic disagreements over direction, particularly in regard to significant issues. You are on the cusp of great success if this ambiguity can be removed. Your record includes a few more wins than losses, but that record could be substantially improved through the removal of this ambiguity. Exposure to a good strategic process would bring considerable value.

Score: 40–69

You are suffering from a severe case of fuzzy vision. There are very differing views of strategic direction among the management team, and this has resulted in erratic operational performance. There are frequent disagreements over strategic issues, and you probably are surprised frequently by competitive tactics. Failure to clear up this ambiguity eventually will lead to even worse operational results. It's time to bring a process into play that will relieve the organization of this ambiguity and stop the bickering.

Score: 1–39

A score in this range indicates too much of a focus on operational issues and short-term results. Decisions are made on an event-by-event basis as opposed to being made within a set of strategic parameters. There is little agreement among the management team over direction, with continuous and heated debates. As a result, decisions frequently are arbitrated and dictated by the CEO in order to break the stalemate. The company is in a me-too strategy mode and is frequently surprised by competitive tactics. Most actions are reactions to competitive initiatives. It is time for a rethink.

AMPLIFICATION OF THE FUZZINESS

And then along comes the Internet! Is your strategy Internet-ready, or will you suffer from strategic fuzziness to the second power?

CHAPTER

3

Strategic Fuzziness²

Most business models can accommodate a constant stream of changes over time. In fact, that is the sign of a successful strategy. Some changes, however, are of such magnitude that they will affect the *structure*, or *genetic code*, of an enterprise and cause a CEO to rethink that business model.

The Internet falls into this category. The shift to a new economy brought on by the advent of the Internet will cause the CEO of *every* company on this planet to rethink its business model. The reason is simple: The Internet will have an impact on *every product, and every customer, in every market, in every industry, in every country*.

To illustrate this point, the following graphic shows the migration of IT since its inception in the late 1960s to the projection that by 2015 over a billion homes will be "wired" through the Internet.

The Internet will be to this century what electricity was to the last century and what steam power was to the one before that. Over the next 50 to 75 years the Internet will infiltrate every nook

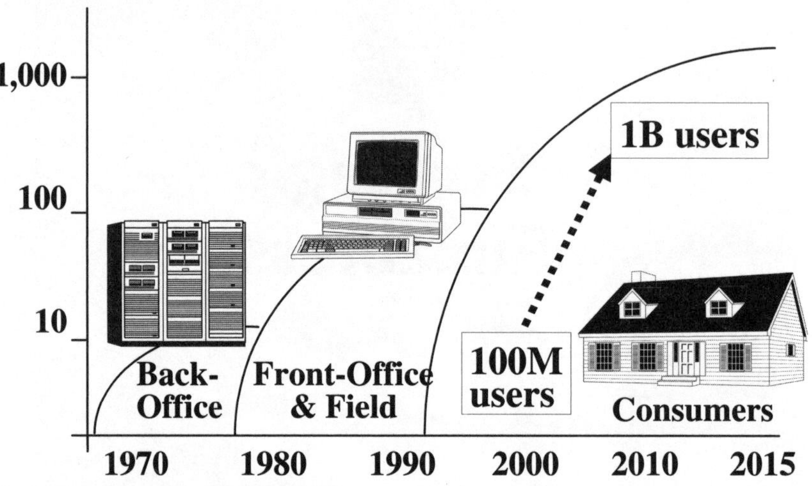

Source: International Data Corporation.

and cranny of society . . . and *business.* Like steam in the nineteenth century and electricity in the twentieth, it will overpower the traditional ways in which we live and conduct business.

In every strategy session in which we have participated in the last three years, the Internet has shown up everywhere: as a threat, an opportunity, a vulnerability, or a critical issue. Most CEOs therefore are conscious of the fact that the Internet will affect their businesses. The dilemma that they all share, however, is: What do we do about it? This question is not about *whether* they should do something but about *what* they should do.

THREE KEY DIFFICULTIES

To most CEOs, the Internet is an *enigma*: They simply don't understand it, and there are not many sources available to help them educate themselves. There are three reasons for this situation:

There are no history books. No one has written any books about his or her experiences with the Internet. It is a change that is happening now—in real time—and it is morphing into something different every day.

There are no experts. In spite of their claims, no consultants have enough experience to be an expert. They are all learning with each new project, usually at a client's expense.

There are no proven models. In spite of the sky-high valuations given to Internet start-ups, the fact remains that none of them has yet withstood the test of time.

The Internet is a "change in progress" and as such has four features that make it very difficult to understand:

- It is *intangible.* Unlike bricks and mortar, which can be seen and even touched, the Internet is intangible. No one can see it or touch it, and as a result, it is seen as something fuzzy and difficult to understand.
- It is a *moving* target. The internet is happening in *real time*, with a constant flow of new applications being found for it every day.
- It is *evolving* every day. Because of the flood of new uses being found of it each day, the Internet is a constant state of flux with an ever-changing profile which will continue to evolve for many years to come.
- It is in a *beta* mode. As was stated above, every application being tried for the Internet is in a laboratory setting where everyone is experimenting, with none of experiments having been completed yet.

Although there is no history, no experience, and no proven models regarding the Internet, the fact is that a CEO has *no choice.* The reason for this is simple: The Internet is a *one-way street.*

The Internet characteristics described above bring with them

NO CHOICE

a major dilemma for the CEO of an enterprise which we call *strategic focus.* Strategic focus is brought to an enterprise through a strategic thinking process which creates a business strategy and enables a CEO to determine the nature of the products the company will offer, the nature of the customers it will pursue, and the nature of the markets it will seek as well as those it will not. This profile becomes the target of the enterprise's business strategy and gives the organization strategic direction and focus.

The Internet, with its intangibility and lack of understanding on the part of most CEOs, can challenge and put into jeopardy the business strategy and focus of an enterprise. The matrix shown in Figure 6 illustrates this phenomenon.

Which quadrant are you in? Our experience from more than 20 years of working with organizations all over the globe, helping them formulate and deploy a *business* strategy, is that most organizations do not have a clear and explicit business strategy. We suspect that the same is true of an Internet strategy, and that leads to *strategic fuzziness squared.*

	BUSINESS CLEAR	**BUSINESS** FUZZY
INTERNET CLEAR	Clear business strategy Clear Internet strategy	Fuzzy business strategy Clear Internet strategy
INTERNET FUZZY	Clear business strategy Fuzzy Internet strategy	Fuzzy business strategy Fuzzy Internet strategy ← STRATEGIC FUZZINESS 2

Figure 6

To determine where your company falls on the above matrix, you may wish to answer another survey.

The Internet Strategy Quotient

1. Do you have an overarching business strategy that guides management decisions?
   ❑Yes 10 ❑No 0
2. Do you have an Internet strategy that is fully integrated and supports your business strategy?
   ❑Yes 10 ❑No 0
3. Do you have an overall "blueprint," designed by your own people, which will determine *where* and *how* the Internet can best be applied in your organization?
   ❑Yes 10 ❑No 0
4. Is your Internet strategy seamless across all the functions of the business?
   ❑Totally 10 ❑Partially 5 ❑No linkage 0
5. Is management on a "crusade," actively promoting your Internet strategy?
   ❑Yes 10 ❑Sometimes 5 ❑No 0
6. Do all the employees understand the Internet strategy and their role in it?
   ❑All do 10 ❑Some do 5 ❑None do 0
7. Are all your key suppliers tied into your Internet strategy?
   ❑All are 10 ❑Some are 5 ❑None are 0
8. Are all your key customers tied into your Internet strategy?
   ❑All are 10 ❑Some are 5 ❑None are 0
9. Which stage are you in with regard to the Internet?
   ❑Fully operational, transactional capability 10
   ❑Some on-line, off-the-shelf transactions 6

❑Nonfunctional Web pages 2
❑No capability 0

10. Are your Internet capabilities fully integrated with your traditional IT systems?
❑Fully 10 ❑Partially 5 ❑None are 0

Total Score___________

Interpretation of the Scores

Score: 75–100

You are in the forefront of management thinking and technological leadership. There are two concerns you should have:

- Since there are no models yet, will ours work?
- Will our competitors learn from us and try to duplicate and improve our system?

To benefit from your "pioneering" efforts, ensure that

- The implementation plan has been screened for potential problems, and actions to prevent those problems have been taken.
- You learn as you implement each piece and reintroduce what you learn into the system to widen your advantage.

Score: 50–75

You have recognized the advent of the Internet and how pervasive it will become throughout society as well as the impact it will have on business. You have decided to try to exploit its use, but not under the umbrella of a coherent corporate Internet strategy. Programs have been instituted on a piecemeal basis, and there has been a lot of trial and error and several unpleasant surprises. One of these surprises might be that the experimentation that is going on does not support the overall business strategy of the organization.

This "piecemeal" approach probably will evolve into incompatible IT systems that will require a lot of costly "retrofitting." The sooner you develop a coherent, integrated Internet strategy that fully supports the corporate strategy, the better off you will be.

Score: 25–50

Your organization has recognized the significance of the advent of the Internet together with the corresponding threats and opportunities it brings. However, you have been reluctant to do anything about it. Most likely, this is the case because there are some components of your business model whose role might be negatively altered and you are agonizing over the consequences.

Do not let this element of your business become an albatross and paralyze decision making. It is during this period of paralysis that your competitors will take market share away from you. Remember that the Internet is here to stay and that if you do not figure out how to exploit it, it will exploit you.

Score: 0–25

You have been so preoccupied with everyday operational issues that you haven't had time to think about what to do about the Internet even though, in the back of your mind, you know it will hit your business someday. You hope, however, that that day is far off. Surprise! It will be sooner than you think.

If you are engrossed in operational issues, it's probably because your corporate strategy is not working. It may be time for a re-think, or maybe it's too late.

Interpretation of the Matrix

Depending where one locates a company on the matrix, a different management solution will be needed.

Fuzzy Business Strategy, Fuzzy Internet Strategy

This is fuzziness to the second power. Overlaying a fuzzy Internet strategy on an already fuzzy business strategy amplifies the ambiguity over direction, thoroughly confuses the employees, and breeds decisions that will cause the organization to meander all over the map. To extract yourself from this situation, you will need both the business strategy and the e-strategy processes described in later chapters of this book.

Fuzzy Business Strategy, Clear Internet Strategy

This is almost an impossible position to be in since it is inconceivable that one can develop a coherent Internet strategy without a clear business strategy to begin with.

Clear Business Strategy, Fuzzy Internet Strategy

Experts who study the fusion of two elements will tell you that the stronger party eventually inherits the other party's weakness and that both parties are brought down to the lowest common denominator. To avoid this situation, you need a catalyst such as the e-strategy process described later in this book.

Clear Business Strategy, Clear Internet Strategy

This is the best situation to be in. There are, as we noted earlier, very few companies in this privileged position.

To get to this position, the first step is to clarify the business strategy of the enterprise. Where you placed your company on the grid indicates whether you should jump into Internet-related programs without a clear Internet strategy or, worse still, without a clear business strategy. Our view is that the Internet, as we will demonstrate in the following chapters, is another tool for deploying a company's business strategy; therefore, an understanding of *that strategy* will shape the Internet strategy.

A review, reconfirmation, or revisit of the business strategy is necessary for another important reason. Lurking in the innards of the Internet is the advent of a new, formidable competitor that your business strategy needs to deal with, and that is the killer.com.

CHAPTER

4

A CEO's Worst Nightmare: Killer.Com

A few years ago, the CEOs of the two dominant book retailers in the United States—Barnes & Noble and Borders—were sitting in their offices, listening to the business news on CNN's *Moneyline* and contemplating ways and means of taking away some of each other's business.

During the newscast, there was a short interview with a gentleman named Jeff Bezos, who declared that he had formed a company named *Amazon.com*, which, effective immediately, would start selling books on-line through the Internet. Furthermore, he stated that Amazon.com would carry over 1 million titles, a hundred times as much as the average bookstore; that the prices would be 30 to 50 percent lower than those in a bookstore; and that a purchase would be made in a couple of minutes from the comfort of one's home simply by using a PC.

A few weeks later, while the CEO of Merrill Lynch was thinking about ways and means to compete with Smith Barney while watching another edition the same program, another young entrepreneur announced the launch of an on-line brokerage company called E-trade.com, which would allow individuals to trade stocks from their home PCs at a fraction of the cost of going through a broker.

Only days later, another Internet entrepreneur announced the start of a company called Priceline.com, which would allow an individual to purchase airline tickets on-line at a price that individual wanted to pay, not at the exhorbitant price that the airlines would want that individual to pay.

Ama . . . who? E . . . who? Price . . . who? Doing . . . what? must have been the reaction of those CEOs on the days of those announcements. All were caught completely off guard by these announcements, and since then, these new Internet companies have become their biggest nightmares.

The day Amazon.com went on-line, Barnes & Nobles' and Borders' business models were put in jeopardy. The day that E-trade.com went on-line, Merrill Lynch's business model of selling stocks through thousands of high-commission salespeople was put in jeopardy. The day that Autobytel.com went on-line, Wayne Huizenga's Autonation business model of selling cars by offering thousands of models displayed on massive car lots was put in jeopardy. The day Jay Walker went on-line with Priceline.com, the entire airline industry's business model was put in jeopardy.

INTRIGUING PHENOMENON

The situations described above, as well as many others which have occurred since that time, bring two intriguing questions:

- Why is it that the business models of dominant enterprises led by astute CEOs can be put in jeopardy overnight?
- What can be done to mitigate or even reverse the impact?

Well-established, dominant enterprises or even an entire industry can be "killed" or seriously injured by a so-called killer.com newcomer because the new economy is conducive to such a phenomenon. As the new economy becomes more and more dependent on *information,* this shift lends itself perfectly to the Internet.

Since the Internet is primarily a *transporter of information,* the more the economy becomes dependent on information, the more disruptive the Internet will be to a business. This is why the companies most threatened by the Internet today are those with a product or service mostly based on information, as shown in the grapic below. These are companies such as those in the banking industry, the insurance industry, the retailing industry, and the stock brokerage industry.

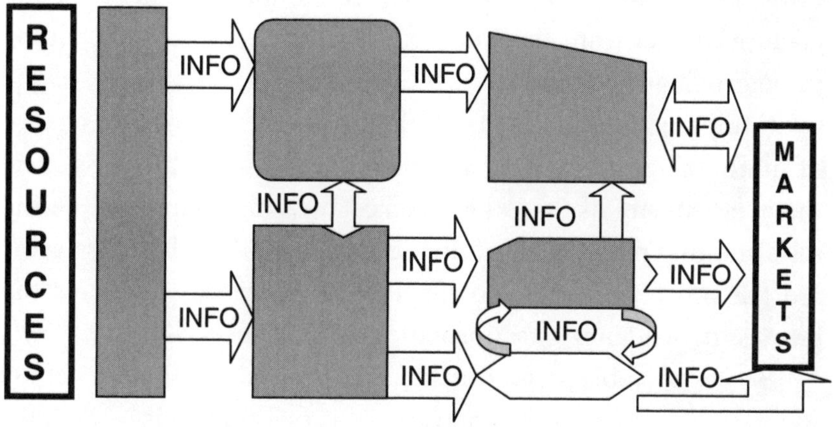

TRADITIONAL VALUE ADDED

Historically, companies in the intangible service industries have added value through a person. Banks help you borrow by having you consult a bank manager who gives verbal advice. Insurance companies have used brokers to give advice to their customers and add value. Stockbrokers have done the same thing through an army of salespeople. In other words, the added value is almost totally dependent on the quality of advice transmitted by a person.

The manufacturers of "hard" goods, by contrast, have attempted to increase value in the product itself by adding more and more physical features. Most of the added value therefore resides in the product itself, and only a small part is based on complementary information.

The new economy is characterized by a value chain that can be fully integrated into the Internet and its supporting cast of technologies, such as servers, routers, mobile computing, wireless communication, ever-increasing bandwidth, and data mining software. This is why "intangible" service companies will suffer the greatest impact from the Internet. Their entire process of adding value is being threatened.

Companies that make "tangible" products have a better chance of minimizing the impact of the Internet on their business since the areas mostly likely to be attacked by a killer.com will be the sales and marketing parts of their business model. These two areas are the most vulnerable to the Internet because they have the greatest dependency on information-laden processes.

Barnes & Noble's traditional business model, created to deploy its strategy, was based on a network of very large stores—so-called bricks and mortar. In this model, information regarding a customer's profile and reading habits is not collected and therefore cannot be recycled to create other services that add value for those customers in other ways in a process that eventually ends with that customer buying more books.

When a person walks into one of those stores, that person's reading preferences are unknown to Barnes & Noble. At Amazon.com, in contrast, that information—and much more—is well known to that company and is held in databases for future use. To date, Amazon.com has this type of information on 17 million of its customers. These databases allow Amazon.com to know exactly the current interests of its customers and their future interests as well.

Simply having each customer's e-mail address allows Amazon.com to do one-to-one selling of new book releases that contain subject matter that the company knows is of interest to each specific customer. This enables Amazon.com to notify each customer when a new book on a particular topic will be available and asks the customer if she or he is interested. In this manner, the company adds value for its customers by supplying *information* that Barnes & Noble cannot provide. This capability gives Amazon.com a tremendous advantage.

THE CONCEPT OF ADDED VALUE^2

Many executives we work with complain that because of the Internet, every product has become a commodity and every transaction is based on price. Our contention, however, is that if every transaction comes down to the lowest price, it is due to two factors:

The customer does not see value.

The customer does not understand the added value.

There basically are two means at your disposal to add value to a product or service. The first is to build features into the product that distinguish it from your competitors' products. The second is to make available to your customers information that enhances their ability to make better decisions while conducting business. Thus, the following equation:

$$\text{Added value}^2 = \text{product features} \times \text{information enrichment}$$

Most executives are quite knowledgeable about how their manufacturing processes add value to their products, but few of them know how *information* can add value for their customers. They understand that the whole organization depends on information, but they don't understand the *flow* of information through the organization and how that information could be made available to customers in ways that would add value and enhance customer relationships. To overcome this difficulty, one must understand the *flow patterns* which route information through the business model together with the interconnectivity of those patterns. One can then use the Internet's capabilities to generate a significant number of applications that provide additional value for customers. These capabilities will be identified in a later chapter.

Added value ⇨ primary features of product or service

Added value ⇨ information enrichment for user

Added value^2 ⇨ primary features × information enrichment → premium prices

As *Business Week* observed in an article about the future impact of the Internet:

> The Internet has the potential to revolutionize the way information and value flow through a business. The biggest profits will go to those that manage Information, not physical assets.[1]

HOW TO AVOID THE KILLER.COM DISRUPTION

This is a key concern which is gaining in importance with more and more CEOs as they see an ever-increasing number of dot-

[1]Adrian J. Slywotzky, "The 21st Century Corporation," *Business Week*, August 28, 2000, pp. 88 and 142.

coms starting up, each targeting a different company or industry. The questions they ask are, Will I be next? and What can I do about it? There are three options available:

1. I can do nothing, wait until someone from Silicon Valley or Seattle creates the killer.com model, and react to it *after* it enters my sandbox.
2. I can call in one of the preeminent consulting firms and pay a fortune for a generic solution that will at best be a "me-too."
3. I can use my own people to develop our own proprietary killer.com model before anyone else does.

Our view is that the third option is the best. However, it requires two elements:

- An understanding of the Internet
- A structured process that works

Any strategy, as was stated earlier, must be oriented toward the *future*. Thus, the first phase in formulating a clear business strategy is to determine what the environment will look like a few years down the road. Let's discuss the elements that make up the future environment of any business.

CHAPTER

5

Back to the Future

Formulating the business strategy of an enterprise is the top item on every CEO's job description. The process of formulating a winning business strategy starts with a CEO envisioning *what* the organization will be in the future and then deploying the resources of the organization in a manner that will make that vision materialize over time. A good strategy should work to the benefit of the organization over a long period of time and be able to deal effectively with the future changes which will present themselves. This implies that the CEO and the management team have thought about what those changes might be. This leads us to ask the following question.

If strategy is about envisioning the organization in the future, why were the CEOs and senior executives of thousands of corporations around the world caught by surprise by the advent of the Internet?

This is the million-dollar question. After all, these are experienced executives who have been successful throughout lengthy careers because of their ability to cope with a multitude of changes, yet with the Internet, most were caught asleep at the switch. An interesting dichotomy.

In our work with the CEOs and executives of our client organizations, we are told repeatedly that changes are happening faster and faster. As a result, they claim, no one can keep up—much less predict anything—especially with the avalanche of changes facing a business today.

Although this claim is partly true, the idea that change happens too quickly to be anticipated is somewhat of a myth. Our work leads us to a different hypothesis. In our view there are two ways to deal with changes: proactively and reactively. Our experience leads us to conclude that most executives deal with most changes in a reactive mode. Their skill is *corrective* in nature rather than being proactive, or *anticipatory*. Our conclusion is that *most executives get caught by surprise because they have not been looking.* When you have not been looking, every change catches you by surprise.

STUCK IN THE CURRENT SANDBOX

A major contributor to the inability of executives to anticipate changes that will affect their businesses is the fact that they are stuck in their *current* sandbox. In other words, they are consumed by what is going on with their *current* products, *current* customers, *current* markets, and *current* competitors. Although this is a necessary element of management, a more important responsibility is to be more concerned about the company's *future* products, *future* customers, *future* markets, and *future* competitors. To be able to change a company's profile, or "look," in any of these areas, one needs to be able to anticipate what the sandbox in which the company will be playing will look like in the *future*, not what it looks like today.

HOW TO ENVISION THE FUTURE BUSINESS ARENA

"How can anyone anticipate what the future sandbox will look like? The future is a *big* place, and no one has a crystal ball." This is usually the next statement we hear after offering our hypothesis. The *business arena* in which a company competes is not one with a limitless number of variables. There are two implicit assumptions in this objection:

1. The future is a big place.
2. One needs a crystal ball to see the future.

Experience has taught us that these are normal objections but that they have a very simple yet rational explanation. It has been shown that many things that look very big and very complex at first sight turn out to be an assembly of a limited number of elements when examined closely. The business arena in which a company competes is such a thing: Although it looks very big and very complex at first, a closer analysis shows that it doesn't have a limitless number of elements.

The business arena in which any company finds itself can be delimited into 12 discrete components:

- Economic environment
- Governmental, political, and regulatory environment
- Social and demographic environment
- Market conditions
- Customer attributes and characteristics
- Competitor profiles
- Technology evolution
- Processing and manufacturing capabilities

- Product design, features, and content
- Sales and marketing methods
- Distribution, delivery, and service methods
- Human, natural, and financial resources

Once the complexity of the future business arena has been analyzed in terms of these 12 "building blocks," one can start to anticipate what the future business arena of any company will look like. This can be accomplished by placing yourself in a "time machine"—moving yourself ahead three to five years and describing the characteristics that each of these elements will have at that point in time. Each of these "parcels" in the sandbox needs to be described *with or without* your company's participation. It is a description of the future business arena that you want to draw a picture of, not a description of your company.

The following questions will achieve this result:

- What will the economic environment in our business arena look like in three to five years?
- What will the governmental, political, and regulatory environment in our business arena look like in three to five years?
- What will the social and demographic environment in our business arena look like in three to five years?
- What will the market conditions in our business arena look like in three to five years?
- What will the customers in our business arena look like in three to five years?
- What will the competitors in our business arena look like in three to five years?
- What will the technology in our business arena look like in three to five years?

- What will processing and manufacturing capabilities in our business arena look like in three to five years?
- What designs, features, and content will products in our business arena have in three to five years?
- What will the sales and marketing methods, and service in our business arena be in three to five years?
- What will be the distribution, delivery methods in our business arena be in three to five years?
- What will the resources (human, natural, and financial) in our business arena look like in three to five years?

Then comes the second objection: "We don't have any futurists in our company. How can we foresee changes that will occur in the future? No one has a crystal ball." The good news is that you don't need guru who reads a crystal ball. We contend submit that most changes that will affect your business 8 to 10 years from now are in place today. Our experience has convinced us that *most changes that affect a company announce themselves well in advance of the time when they will strike.* As John Naisbitt, the renowned futurist, has said: "The best way to predict the future is to understand the present."[1]

In other words, the future is already "folded" into the present, and one must "unfold" it to discover what is on the horizon. You must "go back" to the present to "see the future," as the title of this chapter suggests. But of course, if you have not been looking, you will always be caught by surprise.

THE MYTH OF RAPID TECHNOLOGICAL CHANGE

Many executives think, as we said earlier, that change—particularly technological change—happens faster than they can deal with or faster than can be anticipated. This is somewhat of a myth.

[1]John Naisbitt, Megatrends, Warner Books, 1982, p. 133.

It has been shown that technological change takes 25 to 30 years to find a commercially viable application and another 50 to 70 years to infiltrate all the nooks and crannies of the society that it will eventually affect. However, if you have not been looking, even a change that is creeping along will hit you very quickly. A few examples come to mind.

The first is the invention of electricity. Although electricity was invented in the 1860s, it found a few successful applications only in the 1870s and 1880s. Most of the applications which are now taken for granted were not developed for another two or three decades. This includes street lighting, electric tramways, and the telephone, to mention a few. The same is true of robotics, lasers, and fiber optics; all those technologies were invented in the 1950s but found commercially viable applications some 50 years later.

The microprocessor is another example. Although it was invented in the 1960s and it gave birth to the personal computer in the 1970s, the fact is that in spite of the billions of dollars invested in those products by corporations all over the world, PCs have had a minimal impact on the productivity of those companies. It has been only in the last three to four years that the productive use of PCs has been noticed in this country. Only after some 18 years are we seeing the impact of these machines. In the next 45 years the number of applications will spread disproportionately, and the impact will be felt in almost every home in the country.

The same is true of the Internet. It was invented in 1968 as a backup mechanism for branches of the military to communicate with each other if the regular system was sabotaged by an enemy. It then took some 15 years (the 1980s) to migrate its way to applications in universities and research institutions and then another 10 to 12 years (the late 1990s) to affect industrial companies. How many years is that in total? Our arithmetic comes to a total of 25 to 27 years—pretty close to the standard of other the technologies that preceded it. Now its impact will accelerate and spread itself across society in the same way electricity did. If you have not been looking, especially in the last few years, you will be caught by surprise.

THE THREE FACES OF CHANGE

Changes come in three sizes: *micro, macro,* and *mega.*

Micro changes occur at ground level. These types of changes have limited range and impact. In business, micro changes have an impact on a limited number of products, customers, and markets. When the Italian government decides to privatize a company, that change may have significant implications on Italian industry but most likely will be limited to Italy's borders.

Macro changes can be seen from an airplane at 30,000 feet. These types of changes affect a substantially larger piece of real estate. In business, macro changes affect a large number of products, customers, and markets. Examples of such changes will be discussed later in this chapter.

Mega changes can be seen from a satellite circling the globe and offering a total view of the planet. These types of changes affect *every* product, *every* customer, *every* market, and thus the *structure of every company on this planet.* Obviously, steam power, electricity, and the Internet fall in this category. The next mega change will be discussed later in this chapter.

THE IMPACT OF UNNOTICED MACRO CHANGES

Most executives are so engrossed in ground-level activities that they frequently miss changes that are happening at a higher altitude and that will have a much broader impact on their industry. Mega changes typically happen once in a century while macro changes may be seen once a generation. There are several such changes in play at this moment, many of which have brought effects that have gone unnoticed by most executives. The following are a few of these changes:

- The shift from a push to a pull economy
- The fall of the Berlin wall
- The opening of China
- The demographic dichotomy
- The spread of democracy and capitalism in Latin America
- The fusion of computer and telecommunications technologies

The Shift from a Push to a Pull Economy

This has already occurred, but many executives have not noticed. In a *push* economy, there is more *demand* than *supply* and the *producer* reigns. This was the case from the end of World War II in the mid-1940s until the late 1960s. U.S. companies could sell everything they could make faster than they could make it. Everything they made was gobbled up immediately by long lines of customers fighting each other to buy the few products that were available. In this situation the producer rules the roost. It's Henry Ford's concept that "you can have any car you want, any color you want, as long as it's black." The rationale is simple: If you don't want a black car, step aside because the person behind you will take a black car with no questions asked.

This situation lasted until the early 1970s. Then came the advent of Japanese, Taiwanese, and European manufacturers, which created a situation where today there is more supply than demand in almost every product category. In this situation the *customer* is king, not the producer, and this has changed the rules of play radically, as is illustrated in the following graphic.

ECONOMY	
PUSH	PULL
⇧ DEMAND VS. SUPPLY	⇧ SUPPLY VS. DEMAND
PRODUCER ⇨	CUSTOMER ⇨
MARKET SEGMENTATION	MARKET FRAGMENTATION
LARGER NUMBER OF CUSTOMERS WITH SIMILAR NEEDS	SMALLER NUMBER OF CUSTOMERS WITH DISSIMILAR NEEDS
GENERIC PRODUCT	TAILORED PRODUCT
COMMODITY PRICES	PREMIUM PRICES
LONG PRODUCTION RUNS	SHORTER PRODUCTION RUNS
EFFICIENT MANUFACTURING	FLEXIBLE, EFFECTIVE DECENTRALIZED MANUFACTURING
LONG PRODUCT CYCLES	SHORTER PRODUCT CYCLES
STRONG BRAND LOYALTY	LITTLE BRAND LOYALTY
PERIODIC PRODUCT INNOVATION	CONTINUOUS PRODUCT AND PROCESS INNOVATION
FIXED RULES	CHANGING RULES
STURDY AND STABLE	FAST AND NIMBLE

This change in the nature of economy in which we live will have an impact on a wide array of products, customers, and markets, thus placing it in the macro category.

The Fall of the Berlin Wall

Although this event occurred 12 years ago, the effects are just starting to be seen. Over 220 million people were starving for most of the products that people in America take for granted. As their economic well-being improves, and it will take a generation to do so, the market for "western-type" products will be as large as the Western European market is today.

The Opening of China

In this part of the world, over 1.5 billion people have been without access to the goods the western world enjoys. Again, as their standard of living improves, a population twice the size of those of the United States, Japan, and Western Europe put together will be clamoring for such products. It won't happen without hiccups, but China has opened the door so wide that this change won't be reversed soon. Again, this progression will take a generation to complete itself.

The Demographic Dichotomy

It is a fact today that in the period 2010–2015, almost half the population of the United States will be over 50 years old. Companies which make heavy machinery will have to rethink how to operate those machines. The reason? There will not be enough young, muscle-bound, 23-year-old men who can operate these machines manually. Oil companies will have to rethink the concept of the self-service gas station. The reason? Older people are not as mobile and cannot get out of their cars as easily to help themselves. Maybe, just maybe, having a robot perform that task would relieve people from leaving the comfort of their seats while a car is being refueled.

The dichotomy, however, is this: The rest of the world is going the other way. Mexico, most of South America, and most of Asia will have 50 percent of their populations under the age of 25. These demographic changes and the dichotomy they bring will affect any product that is "global" in nature. And *today* is the time to be thinking about this, not 8 to 10 years from now.

The Spread of Democracy and Capitalism in Latin America

The spread of democracy and capitalism in Brazil, Argentina, and Chile will bring another 200 million people into the western economy.

The Fusion of Computer and Telecommunications Technologies

The fusion of computer and telecommunications technologies, which started some 30 years ago, will accelerate and have an impact on an ever-increasing number of products, customers, and markets.

The other aspect of these macro changes is that they are all converging on CEOs and their management teams at the same time. Which school of management will you fall into? The reactive, after-the-fact, corrective mode or the proactive, when-it's-timely, anticipatory mode?

MEGA CHANGES

Mega changes usually present themselves once a century. However, in the last 20 years we have been hit by two mega changes, both of which were born in the late 1960s and are poised to spread their impact across society over the next 50 years. One is obviously the Internet; the other is a science called *biotech*.

Although the "buzz" these days is all about the Internet, our view is that biotech will affect every product, every customer, and every market. As a *transporter* of information, the Internet will affect the information flow patterns of businesses and consumers. Biotech, however, will penetrate the human body. To help a patient with Parkinson's disease control severe tremors, the company known as Medtronic is developing a device which will consist of a drug on a chip that will be gently inserted into the brain, where it will emit electrical signals that will stop the tremors. Just as a car now has an average of 30 chips, experts are predicting that in 10 to 15 years the human body will have that many biochips.

A CEO's first priority is to formulate, articulate, and communicate the *business strategy* of the enterprise. That strategy must allow the company to accommodate most changes, *including* the Internet.

The process required to help a CEO formulate a winning business strategy, which we call strategic thinking, is not, unfortunately, a prevelant skill among executives.

CHAPTER

The First Imperative: Clarifying the Business Strategy

Our firm has been involved in the field of strategy since the mid-1970s. Back then there was an explosion of literature on the subject of strategy, and we started browsing through those books to get an understanding of what the term meant. Unfortunately, we became more confused than educated. The reason was simple. Each author who wrote about this subject used the word *strategy* with a different meaning. One author described strategy as the "objective" and tactics as the "means." The next author defined the objective as the "goal" and the strategy as the "means." These two definitions are 180 degrees apart in meaning. The next author claimed that strategy is "long-term" thinking whereas tactics is "short-term" thinking. In other words, this author differentiated between the two modes of thinking on the basis of time.

The second element we noticed in those books was that most of them were written by academic people who almost never spoke or worked with the companies they wrote about. In fact, their formulas were developed by trying to re-create, as outsiders looking in, the "magic recipe" a particular company had followed to become successful and then publish a book about their so-called findings.

Our approach was a different. We said to ourselves: Let's go out and talk to *real* people who run *real* organizations. Let's find out what strategy means to them and how they go about determining the future of their businesses. We went out and started talking to CEOs in a variety of different industries, of different sizes, and in different countries. Eventually we even participated in the meetings these CEOs had with their people when they wrestled with the issue of strategy. The process described in this chapter therefore, did not come out of the blue but was extracted from the heads of *real* people running *real* companies.

What you will find in this chapter are the concepts and key ideas we heard these people discussing and debating. The process we describe is a reflection of the thinking patterns that we saw these CEOs use, and that is why we use the term *strategic thinking.*

THE CURE FOR STRATEGIC FUZZINESS^2

Since our experience has demonstrated that most companies have an implicit strategy, the first step in avoiding strategic fuzziness squared is to make that strategy *explicit.* It is imperative that any ambiguity about the *future direction* of a company be removed before that company launches an Internet initiative.

STRATEGY STARTS WITH A VISION

The first observation we made, when talking to a CEO about the future of a business was that every CEO had a "vision" of what he or she wanted the company to look like at some point in the future.

Basically, the CEO employed and deployed the assets of the company in pursuit of that vision.

Strategic thinking, then, is the type of thinking that occurs inside the head of the CEO and the members of the management team, who attempt to transform this vision into a profile of what they want the company to look like at some point in the future.

Strategic thinking is similar to picture painting. It involves putting the management team in a room and having them paint or draw a picture or profile of what they want the organization to look like at some time in the future.

This vision or profile becomes the target for all decisions and plans. Plans and decisions that fall within the frame of that picture are pursued and those outside the frame are not. In other words, you want to give your people a filter that will help them make *intelligent and consistent decisions over time.* This leads to another question: "If I am to draw a picture of what I want the company

to look like in the future in order to help my people make better decisions, what do I include in the picture?"

THE STRATEGIC PROFILE OF AN ENTERPRISE

A company's "profile" consists of four elements:

- The scope of its products
- The scope of its customers
- The scope of its industry segments
- The scope of its geographic markets

All the other things used by management, such as selling methods, distribution channels, and manufacturing processes, are *inputs* to the construction of this profile or *outputs* such as profit and returns.

Therefore, if the CEO wants to guide the direction of the company and influence its eventual look, he or she must determine in advance, not only which products, customers, market segments, and geographic markets the company will pursue but, more important, which products, customers, market segments, and geographic markets it will *not* pursue.

Strategically, it is more important to know what the strategy *does not* lend itself to than what it does. The reason is simple: Management makes two types of decisions that over time shape the look of the business in these four areas. The first is how it *allocates resources*, and the second is how it *chooses opportunities.* Using the strategic profile as a filter will cause management to allocate resources and choose opportunities that are on the "more emphasis" side in the accompanying graphic as opposed to those on the "less emphasis" side.

The next question that surfaces is: What determines the line of demarcation between items that should receive more emphasis

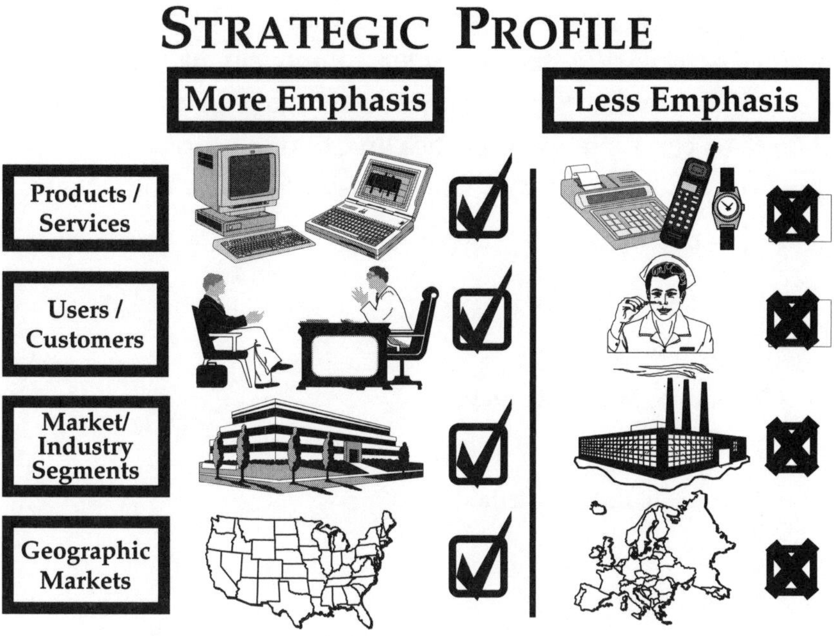

STRATEGIC PROFILE

	More Emphasis	Less Emphasis
Products / Services	✓	✗
Users / Customers	✓	✗
Market/ Industry Segments	✓	✗
Geographic Markets	✓	✗

and those which should receive less? The answer to this question is a *fundamental* concept of strategy that we call the *driving force.*

IDENTIFY THE DRIVING FORCE OF THE BUSINESS

The true test to determine whether a company has a strategy is to watch how management goes about deciding whether to pursue an opportunity. What we observed was that management would take the opportunity through a hierarchy of different filters but that the *ultimate* filter was always whether there was a fit between the products, customers, and markets the opportunity brought and *one* key component of the business. If management found a good fit there, it would pursue that opportunity; if it did not, it would not pursue it. However, that one component of the business used as a filter was different from one company to the next.

In each company, one component seemed to be pushing, propelling, or *driving* it forward. *One* component of the business seemed to dominate management's thinking in allocating resources or choosing opportunities. In exploring this concept further, we found that any company consists of 10 basic components:

- Product or service
- Customer or user class
- Market category
- Technology or know-how
- Production capability or capacity
- Sales or marketing method
- Distribution method
- Natural resources
- Size or growth
- Return or profit

Although all these components are present in every business, one is at the root of a company, and knowing which one that is vital to management's ability to make consistent decisions.

THE CONCEPT OF THE DRIVING FORCE

Product-Driven Strategy

A product-driven company is one that has deliberately limited its business to a *single* product. As a result, future products are very predictable because they will be modifications, extensions, or adaptations of the current product, which is also a linear, genetic extrapolation of the original product. Coca-Cola and "Coke" soda are a good example. Firestone and tires are another. Harley Davidson and motorcycles are a third.

Customer or User Class–Driven Strategy

A customer or user class–driven company is one that has deliberately restricted its business to a *describable* class of customer or end user. The company then looks to satisfy certain specific needs these people have and the responds with a wide variety of genetically unrelated products. Johnson & Johnson's, strategy of satisfying the "health needs of doctors, nurses, patients, and mothers" has led the company into a broad array of genetically *unrelated* products all of which are targeted at those four user groups.

Market Category–Driven Strategy

A market category–driven company is one that has deliberately decided to target its strategy at a specific market and respond with a broad array of products that all are aimed at that market. American Hospital Supply is an example of this type of company.

Technology-Driven Strategy

A technology-driven company has a basic or distinctive technology or expertise at the root of its business. This type of company then looks for potential applications of that technology, around which it then designs its products. Companies such as Dupont, 3M, and Dow Corning are good examples.

Production Capability or Capacity–Driven Strategy

A capacity-driven company is one that has a substantial investment in its production facility and whose strategy is to fill the capacity to its maximum. Paper mills, steel mills, and refineries are good examples.

A production capability–driven company is one that has built into its production process some distinctive capabilities that allow it to give its products features that other competitors have difficulty replicating. Specialty steel producers and specialty printers are examples of companies with this driving force.

Sales or Marketing Method–Driven Strategy

A sales or marketing method–driven company hs a *unique* or *distinctive* method of selling to or getting orders from its customers. All the products the customers buy must be sold through that method, and all the markets the company enters must allow it to utilize that method. Door-to-door selling and companies such as Mary Kay, Avon, and Tupperware are good examples.

Distribution Method–Driven Strategy

A company distribution method–driven has a *unique* or *distinctive* method of moving things or matter from one place to another, and all the opportunities it pursues must utilize that distribution system. FedEx, Wal-Mart, and telephone and railroad companies are good examples.

Natural Resources–Driven Strategy

In natural resources–driven companies, the pursuit of and access to natural resources determine how a company allocates its capital and what opportunities it chooses. Examples are major oil companies such as Exxon and Shell and mining companies such as Newmont and Broken Hill Properties.

Size or Growth or Return or Profit–Driven Strategy

In these two categories we find the financial conglomerates such as GE, Allied-Signal, and Danaher.

STRATEGIC QUESTIONS

To determine if your strategy is clear or fuzzy, you may want to think about the following questions:

- Which of the driving forces described above is the current heartbeat of your business and the root of your strategy?
- Which driving force would each of your subordinates say is at the root of your strategy and a filter for your decisions?

Experience has shown that different people have different perceptions about which component is the driving force of a strategy. Unfortunately, this results in decisions that cause a company to zigzag its way forward.

Once there is agreement about the current driving force, another set of key questions needs to be asked:

- Which component *should* drive the strategy in the future?
- Should we continue to be driven as we have been or should we be exploring another driving force?
- If we explore another driving force, which one should it be?
- What implications will that driving force have on the products, customers, and markets we pursue and the ones we don't?
- What will the company look like if we change to a different driving force?

It is the quality of the answers to these questions that makes the driving force a fundamental concept of strategy.

FORMULATING A STRATEGY AROUND THE DRIVING FORCE OF THE ENTERPRISE

To us, the words *strategy, mission, charter, mandate, business purpose,* and *business statement* are all synonymous. If one were to browse through the annals of business history books, one would be told by author after author that on any day of its existence, every corporation has a *strategy at the root of its business.* In other words, an underlying business strategy is being practiced by the management of any organization, although that strategy may not be apparent to the members of the organization.

Alfred Sloan, who was the CEO of General Motors in the first half of this century, put it this way in his book *My Years with General Motors*:

> Every enterprise needs a concept of its industry. There is a logical way of doing business in accordance with the facts and circumstances of an industry, if you can figure it out. If there are different concepts among the enterprises involved, these concepts are likely to express competitive forces in their most vigorous and most decisive forms.[1]

Peter Drucker, the guru of all management gurus, calls it the "theory of the business." In a 1994 *Harvard Business Review* article, he outlined his thesis:

> Every organization, whether a business or not, has a *theory of the business.* Indeed, a valid theory that is clear, consistent, and focused is extraordinarily powerful. These are the assumptions that shape any organization's behavior, dictate its decisions about what to do and what not to do, and define what the organization considers meaningful results. These assumptions are about markets. They are about identifying customers and competitors, their values, and the

[1]Alfred P. Sloan, *My Years with General Motors*, Doubleday, 1972, p. 42.

company's strengths and weaknesses. These assumptions are about what a company gets paid for. They are what I call a company's *theory of the business.*[2]

Our view on the subject of strategy statements is simple:

- A good strategy statement should not be longer than a paragraph or two. There is no need to have pages and pages describing what the business is about. However, every word, modifier, and qualifier must be carefully thought through because each one moves the line of demarcation between the products, customers, and markets that will receive more emphasis and those which will receive less.
- The ability of people to execute a CEO's strategy is inversely proportionate to the length of the strategy statement.

HOW TO CONSTRUCT A MEANINGFUL STRATEGY STATEMENT

A *strategy statement* that can serve the executives of a corporation as a test bed to make consistent and intelligent decisions on behalf of the company must contain the following elements:

- The first sentence must clearly describe *the* driving force of the organization. In other words, it must isolate the specific component of the business that gives the company a *strategic and distinctive advantage* over its competitors. If a company is product-driven, what is the specific product that drives the business? If a company is technology-driven, which specific technology is at the root of the business? If a company is production capability–driven, which specific production capability drives the business?

[2]Peter Drucker, "The Theory of the Business," *Harvard Business Review*, September/October 1994.

- The second part of the statement should contain words—nouns, adjectives, qualifiers, and modifiers—that delineate the line of demarcation between the "nature" of the products, customers, market segments, and geographic markets to which the driving force lends itself and the nature of those to which it does not.
- The statement should have a "tone" of growth, since growth is a given in business. Every business must grow in order to perpetuate itself.
- It must have a tone of success, as success is naturally implied from a sound strategy.
- Finally, it must reflect *future intent* and present condition. The statement should give people a feel for what it will be in the *future*, not what it is today.

Depending on the driving force, each strategy statement will be dramatically different.

EXAMPLES OF STRATEGY STATEMENTS

The following are examples of strategy statements we have helped our client organizations construct. For reasons of confidentiality, the names of the companies have been omitted. In each instance, the driving force appears in italics.

The first example is from a product-driven company:

> Our strategy is to market, manufacture, and distribute *saw blade products* made from strip metal stock that provide exceptional value.
>
> We will concentrate on high-performance, material separation applications where we can leverage our integrated manufacturing capabilities to develop customized, innovative, consumable products with demonstrable advantages that bring premium prices.
>
> We will seek customer segments and geographic markets where

> the combination of superior distribution and technical support services will give us an additional competitive advantage.

The next one is a user class–driven concept:

> We proactively seek out the building, repair, and remodeling needs of *professional trades people and DIYers* in the commercial and residential construction industry.
>
> We respond with cost-effective, differentiated staple products that enhance the performance or ease the installation of key building materials.
>
> We concentrate in geographic markets with a growing construction industry and an adequate distribution infrastructure to reach a critical mass of end users.
>
> Our intent is to be the recognized leader in the industry.

The following example is from a production capability–driven company.

> Our strategy is to leverage our cutting-edge, integrated *specialty textile manufacturing capability* to exploit interior service applications for which we can develop customized, differentiated products.
>
> We will target and strive to dominate market niches that offer above-average margins/profit.
>
> We will seek geographic markets with high growth potential where our superior sales, distribution, and service skills bring an additional competitive advantage.

Exotic? Definitely not! Sexy? Absolutely not! Powerful? You bet! The purpose of a clear strategy statement is not to arouse people but to give them a clear sense of direction and equip them with a tool to make intelligent and consistent decisions on behalf of the organization. In the next section we explain how the business concept is used to screen opportunities.

TURNING THE STRATEGY STATEMENT INTO A STRATEGIC FILTER

The following statement is from another of our clients:

> Our strategy is to leverage our *multipurpose, continuous process capability to combine metals and polymers to produce and market multilayered structures.*
>
> We will proactively seek out applications where we can respond with differentiated products that add value, are tailored to the specific needs of customers and end users, and bring cost, performance, and/or quality competitive advantages
>
> We will concentrate in growth-oriented industry segments in which we can be a leader and in geographic markets where there are multiple applications available to us.

Although this strategy statement sounds highly technical, it can be transformed into a very effective and simple *binary* filter to screen opportunities that come to the business. One simply takes an opportunity through a series of questions which demand a yes or no answer, as illustrated by the accompanying Strategic Filter questionnaire.

The more "checks" the opportunity receives on the "no" side of the ledger, the larger the red flag should become, because that opportunity is violating major aspects of the strategy of the business.

THE CONCEPT OF AREAS OF EXCELLENCE

Over time, the strategy of an organization can, like a person, get stronger and healthier or get ill and weak. What determines whether the strategy gets stronger are the *areas of excellence*, or strategic capabilities, an organization deliberately nurtures to a higher level of proficiency than *any* competitor can.

Strategic Filter

Does the opportunity	Yes	No
• Leverage *and/or enhance* our multipurpose continuous process capability to combine *metals* and *polymers*?	❑	❑
• Produce *multilayered* structures?	❑	❑
• Provide an ability to respond with differentiated products that add value?	❑	❑
• Provide products tailored to the specific needs of customers?	❑	❑
• Bring		
Cost advantages?	❑	❑
Performance advantages?	❑	❑
Quality advantages?	❑	❑
• Target a growth-oriented industry sector?	❑	❑
• Bring geographic markets with multiple applications?	❑	❑
• Allow us to be a leader?	❑	❑

Another key observation we made some years ago is that these areas of excellence change dramatically from one driving force to another. A product-driven company, for instance, needs to excel in two areas: product development and sales or service. A customer class–driven company must excel at two very different skills: customer research and customer loyalty. A production capacity–driven company must excel and be more *efficient* than any competitor and also excel at *substitute marketing.*

The following graphics illustrate the relationship between the driving force of the strategy and the corresponding areas of excellence.

No company has the resources to "outexcel" all its competitors across all these capabilities. Thus, there is a need to identify which skills support the driving force of the strategy so that, in allocating resources, these areas get *preferential* treatment during good times and bad times.

Understanding the driving force and the areas of excellence

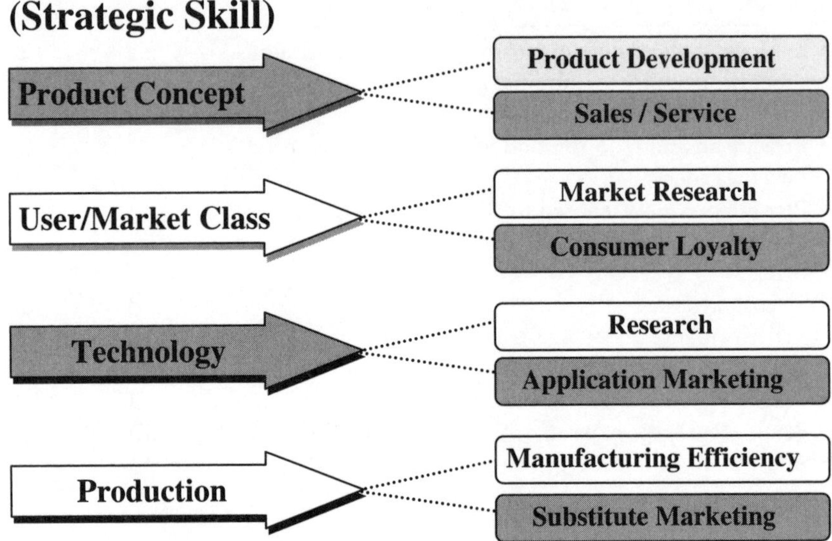
AREAS OF EXCELLENCE
(Strategic Skill)
Product Concept
Product Development
Sales / Service
User/Market Class
Market Research
Consumer Loyalty
Technology
Research
Application Marketing
Production
Manufacturing Efficiency
Substitute Marketing

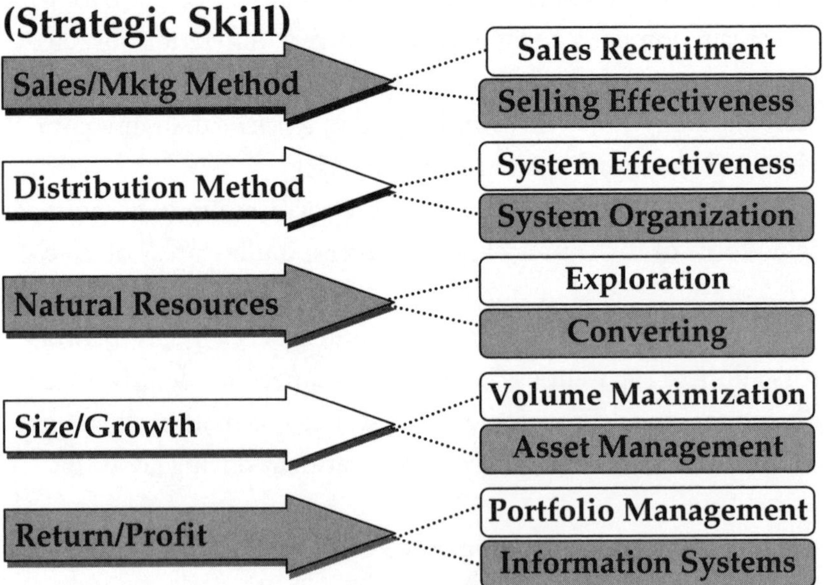
AREAS OF EXCELLENCE
(Strategic Skill)
Sales/Mktg Method
Sales Recruitment
Selling Effectiveness
Distribution Method
System Effectiveness
System Organization
Natural Resources
Exploration
Converting
Size/Growth
Volume Maximization
Asset Management
Return/Profit
Portfolio Management
Information Systems

makes it possible to project and determine which products, customers, and markets lend themselves to these areas and which ones do not.

MANAGE YOUR COMPETITOR'S STRATEGY TO YOUR ADVANTAGE

Most companies that want to grow in today's environment must do so at a competitor's expense. We at DPI are firm believers that the concepts of driving force and areas of excellence can be applied to each of your competitors and that their strategy can be uncovered. Once this is known, you can initiate certain actions to manage your competitors' business as well as your own and grow at their expense.

Different competitors may have different driving forces and thus behave differently in similar circumstances. This is contrary to the accepted wisdom, which says that all competitors in an industry behave in the same manner. We have never found that to be true.

General Motors (GM) and Honda are both in the automobile industry. However, while GM makes only cars and trucks, Honda also makes motorcycles, robots, lawn mowers, and generators. Thus, GM pursues a *product-driven* strategy while Honda pursues a *technology-driven strategy*. Honda focuses on providing "engines for the world," while GM offers a "car for each income stratum."

CHANGE THE RULES OF PLAY

Never play the game the way your competitor plays the game. In other words, you do not grow at a competitor's expense by imitating that competitor's strategy. *Imitation may the finest form of flattery, but it is the worst form of strategy*. Instead, you must *neutralize that strategy by changing the rules of play*.

In 1980 Xerox had 98 percent of the worldwide copier market;

in 1985 it had 12 percent. Why? Canon came into the business and completely changed the rules. Instead of offering large machines, it introduced small ones; instead of selling direct, it went through distributors; and instead of leasing a machine, it sold it outright. It took Xerox five years to decide to go through distributors and seven years to wean itself from its leasing program—86 market share points too late!

IDENTIFY THE CRITICAL ISSUES

Many times we have seen a good strategy not be successful because the implications of that strategy were not anticipated and the *critical issues* for managing those implications were not successfully identified. Thus, the last key concept of strategic thinking is to identify the critical issues that will need to be managed and resolved to make the strategy work.

These critical issues become the "work plan" for management since they are the *bridge* that will take the organization from what it looks like today to what it wants to look like tomorrow.

Critical Issue 1: The Internet

If your current method of strategy formulation has not surfaced the advent of a killer.com competitor in your business arena, you are using the wrong process. In every strategy session we have facilitated in the last two or three years, the Internet has been in the top two of the six to eight critical issues that usually surface in any session. The reason is simple. The Internet brings migraine headaches to a CEO. The Internet, as the *ultimate e-nigma*, can be understood only if one understands its distinctive capabilities.

From File Folders to Digital File Transfer

Interview:
Philip C. Kantz,
President and CEO,
TAB Products

Remember the paperless office? Predictions in the early 1980s said that by now we'd all have a clean desk with nothing but a computer on it. Needless to say, it didn't happen that way: The computer has generated more paper than ever. That's good news for TAB Products Co., Inc., of Palo Alto, California, which is in the business of managing documents and making the information in them accessible quickly on paper, electronically, or otherwise.

Phil Kantz, the CEO of TAB, warns that "there was a study about three years ago indicating that while paper documents as a percentage of total documents will drop from 90 to 30 percent in the next 10 years, the absolute number of paper documents will grow by a factor of four."

In all that paper lies the future of TAB, best known for its color-coded folders and labels invented by two ex-IBM-ers in the late 1940s. Those folders and products, along with the cabinets used to hold them and the furniture used by the people handling them, sustained TAB's business for more than 50 years. TAB was comfortable in its position as a premium provider of those products to document-intensive industries such as insurance, health care, and financial services, but growth and profits were getting tougher to come by as its products became increasingly subject to competition and commoditization. When Phil Kantz became CEO in 1997, he envisioned a very different future for TAB:

> When I first took this job in January 1997, one of our senior executives asked me why I'd come to TAB. I said that there are three external factors and three internal factors. The first external factor is that this is a very interesting space that you guys are in called information management, but you haven't looked at it that way.
>
> The second thing is that outsourcing is a key trend. That is to say, managing documents of any kind, paper or otherwise, is never considered a strategic core competency of a company. Take insurance, for example. They have underwriting or product development as core competencies, so they'll outsource things like document management to the guys who do it really well.
>
> And the third factor was globalization, in which large companies like to deal with large companies. So here we were, a company that had, literally, a global presence but wasn't using it for anything.
>
> Then there are the internal issues relevant to this question. First, this company was 50 years old, and it actually had a well-known brand name. Second, although TAB had $150 million in sales, they'd done it two years in a row, so the business wasn't growing. The third thing that became obvious to me was that it was a very product-focused business, and they were in danger of getting commoditized out. And then I found out that the company really had no strategy. I asked a number of people right after I got here what the strategy was, and the answer was, "Sell, sell, sell."

Throughout most of his career Kantz has specialized in what he calls transformations, and in TAB he saw a golden opportunity not to do a "turnaround" but to *transform* the way TAB's people looked at the company. He elected to use DPI's strategic thinking process to facilitate that transformation. As Kantz explains,

A transformation is exactly what it says: a changing of the form. In a turnaround you're tweaking things, cutting costs, fixing things. In a transformation you make more fundamental changes in what the company actually does and how it views itself. What I was looking for was a framework for contextualizing the transformation, a process that other people could grab on to. And one of the things that I've found over time is that you could be really good at this as a CEO, but if you also try to be the one who imposes the process and be the facilitator, it doesn't work.

What happens is, the very silos you're trying to overcome are exacerbated. The people that have been around a while take everything personally. You're going to be changing all the things that they did. By definition, they must be wrong. All the new people start to feel they're on the good team. All the longer-tenured people feel they're on the wrong team.

When you bring in the framework and facilitation provided by the strategic thinking process, your objective is to bring these disparate groups together without any bias or categorization. Then it doesn't make any difference whether you've been here a month or thirty-three years. You can still contribute. It doesn't make any difference whether your background is as an MBA or a high school dropout. A lot of people think you need forty years in business or an MBA from Harvard to be able to strategize. That couldn't be farther from the truth. The framework that DPI has developed enables people who have just a basic understanding of doing business to understand the process and, importantly, to feel like they're contributing to that process. It brings everyone to the same level, regardless of disparate educational backgrounds. So I really like it. It *demystifies* the concept of strategy.

The second thing is its focus on execution. It puts the right things in front of you. You know what your driving force is. There's

> a new business concept that develops from the driving force. There are strategic capabilities that flow out of the new business concept and the driving force. And from those comes a strategic filter for decision making that constantly reinforces the process of executing the strategy. I appreciate that because that's one of the things leadership has to do.
>
> I read an article a number of years ago, and I think it was Peter Drucker who wrote: "You can't be a good leader unless you have a good follower." Part of having good followers is making sure that they're on board with what you're doing and why you're doing it, what their role is, what's in it for them, what's in it for the company, and what's in it for the customer. The process allows you to articulate all of that within a single framework.

As the TAB management team went through the strategic thinking process, a new picture of the company's future began to form. During the selection of the future driving force, for example, the individual work groups were surprised to find that they unanimously agreed that they should not be product-driven, that their new driving force should be document management know-how. This decision would have far-reaching implications for the company, affecting the products, services, markets, and customers it would pursue in the future—and those it would not.

As Kantz explains it,

> The driving force is not intuitive, oddly enough. I think it's a unique part of the process and naturally leads to the identification of the strategic capabilities important to the business. Interestingly, I think that without this process we wouldn't have concluded that the strategic capabilities are what they are. We probably would have decided on a different set of capabilities and over the next two or three years, by trial and error, come to the same conclusions the strategic think-

> ing process helped us see. Through the process we could clearly see them right away.
>
> We also have made extensive use of the strategic filter, which is one of the outputs of the process. It becomes easy to negotiate day in and day out. We thought about this constantly and continue to do so. When you finish the process, that filter has been constructed and agreed to by everybody in the room. Nobody can go away saying that this filter was just developed by the new guys or this filter was developed by the people who had been around a long time. No, actually it was developed by *us*, and we're all on the same team. And nobody could leave that room and say, "I didn't agree with that." Because as soon as somebody would say, "Well, I'm not so sure that that's right," the facilitator would say, "Stop. Let's go back and revisit it, because we're not leaving this room until we've agreed on this."

As TAB has moved forward to bring its future profile to fruition, the strategic filter has become an integral part of management's thinking and has helped guide it through some crucial changes in the business.

Says Kantz,

> I'll give you an example that actually came out of the process. We had a small business in maintenance, repair, and warranty service of electromechanical devices called optical disk storage jukeboxes, manufactured by others. TAB had started this business maybe 20 years ago. The problem was that since we decided to be a know-how–driven company, focused on document management, it no longer fit. It's a very different type of business. We tried like hell to *make* it fit. Another output of the process is identifying not only what things should receive more emphasis but also what things *shouldn't* be emphasized as much. This business was on the "less emphasis" list, but it had all the profit return metrics that we wanted to achieve, and now it didn't look like a strategic fit. We thought

> maybe that wasn't right. Maybe we needed to focus more on it. We looked at it and saw that imaged documents are stored on these jukeboxes. So maybe there was a back end in. Maybe because these guys deal with executives and management in the data-processing departments and information technology departments of big companies, maybe there's a great opportunity to deal with the mahogany door sell but also have somebody at the back door, and those two groups would communicate and plan together. We tried for a year and couldn't get it to work. Last year we sold the business. It just didn't make sense. We found a company that really did see it as being in the mainstream of its strategy, and they were willing to pay more to keep our people, to keep our management team. It was the right decision for both of us.

As TAB has progressed over the past year, many more changes have taken place, such as the deemphasis of its forms-handling-equipment business and substantial growth in its professional services unit. The company's profits are up about 20 percent on professional services. The transformation, in Kantz's view, has been greatly eased by the depth of understanding and commitment to the new picture of TAB's future strategic profile:

> We've already made an enormous number of changes. Choosing a driving force did a number of things, because you can't focus on the driving force without focusing on the strategic capabilities. In coming to grips with that we were able to look back in our history and come to closure on what the company *really did* for its customers rather than on the *products* it provided to its customers. What we found was that we were in fact a pioneer in the field of records management and that over time, the best relationships we developed were the result of solutions that we sold to our customers which happened to drag along our products and services rather than customers wanting to buy just another folder, label, piece of furniture,

> or filing cabinet. One of the things the process helped us do was understand the importance of what I call the underpinnings of the technology strategy, our solutions in records management, and our consultative selling approach to our customers.

As a "transformation" specialist, Kantz is aware that this kind of basic shift in the business takes three to four years to mature. However, he believes that in less than two years, irreversible momentum has taken hold and significant progress has been made:

> Today, thanks to the strategic thinking process, we are a document management company. That means we can sell many of the same products and services as before, but now we have a focus. We're experts at managing paper-based files, records, and documents—information, if you will. But now we have a little bit of a twist, which is recognizing the convergence that's going on among paper, image, and electronic documents. We provide access to the information that's embedded in that paper at the desktop for our clients. We have become a technology company in terms of our driving force and help our customers move from one medium to another with the simple objective of getting access to information.

Delivering over the Internet

Accessing information today inevitably involves the Internet, which, because of the nature of TAB's business, will be an important part of the company's future.

Phil Kantz, as a director and board member of several well-known Silicon Valley firms, is more Net-savvy than most. When he saw the potential role of the Internet in TAB's future, he realized the need to raise the level of understanding among his key managers and develop an e-strategy that would fully support TAB's ongoing transformation. He decided to use DPI's e-strategy process to accomplish those results.

Says Kantz,

> We didn't have an Internet strategy, but TAB understands that the world is changing because of the Internet. While we were in the midst of the company's transformation, we wanted to make sure we were putting the Internet into its proper perspective. The goal was simple: to consider and plan for the Internet's impact on our business and on our know-how driving force. So the whole idea of going through the e-strategy process was first to bring everyone's awareness level up to the same degree. I probably have a more significant level, because of my involvement in the industry, than anybody else in the company. So one of the things we challenged the management team to do was to get up to speed on the Internet, understand what was going on out there, and step away from the transformation for a few days to focus on those new technologies and what they could mean for us. That could mean either a competitor coming in and upsetting the very transformation that we had under way or identifying the things that *we* could use in the transformation to get a competitive advantage.
>
> The e-strategy process gave me a chance to get the group together. I wasn't sure exactly how to do it in a way that it would be not "The sky is falling" but "Gee, we're saying our mission is to help our customers get access to critical information in documents from paper to the desktop. And you can't talk about the desktop today without talking about the World Wide Web, without acknowledging the importance of the Internet technology itself."

As Kantz points out, a major obstacle to developing an Internet strategy at most companies are the varying levels of understanding of the Internet among the members of top management and the lack of a "common language" with which to approach the subject.

To that end, the people at TAB found the 12 e-nablers to be invaluable in bringing management up to speed on the Internet and how it applies to various business and information processes.

In Kantz' view, "One of the most valuable aspects of the e-strategy process is these e-nablers. Those concepts brought our entire executive team up to the same level of awareness about the Internet, its potential impacts, and the nomenclature of the Web."

Based on that new understanding and a strong commitment to the "transformation strategy," the management team could use the process to immediately identify some crucial components of its future with the Internet, including the establishment of an alliance with a key software developer. TAB had come to the realization that it could be *the* leader in delivering archived documents quickly and inexpensively to customers over the Internet.

In line with this objective, says Kantz, "The most important output of the e-strategy process for us was the decision to move even more aggressively than we had been in aligning with a partner in EDMS [electronic data management software]."

Three Key Decisions

If one follows the company's train of thought over the last year, one can see that a clear conversion has taken shape from the old business model to the new. Kantz explains:

> We made three major decisions that will change the shape of TAB. The first action we took was to sell our old field services business. The second action was to recognize the importance of imaging to us, especially in situations where we could deal exclusively with electronic imaging output. Typically, what we do now is take documents from any medium—it could be a microform, microfiche, microfilm, something like that, or it could be paper or even an electronic im-

> age—and convert them to an electronic deliverable that is readable by any one of the many document management platforms. It could be FileNet, IBM, or whatever. Typically, our output would be a CD-ROM or a magnetic form, and that becomes the deliverable. We decided early on, as we got involved with the various conversion technologies, that that was the place we wanted to play—electronic output, any medium to electronic output of an imaged document. And so we ended up buying the operations of a company in Texas called Docucon. As a matter of fact, we just closed the transaction at the end of May. And that was a key part of it, because we had about a year's worth of involvement with imaging and got a sense of what it was and how important it was going to be to our paper-to-the-desktop strategy.

It became clear to Kantz at that stage that the next logical step was to deliver imaged documents over the Internet. In the middle of the e-strategy process, the urgency of the issue became apparent, and a step they had been looking at quickly rose to the top as a high-priority item:

> It is important to realize that we didn't *have* an Internet strategy going into the process. So we came away with an understanding that we could be successful with our transformation but lose the battle to Internet innovators unless we implemented the e-strategy we developed and did it swiftly. We determined that we needed to move faster with a key strategic software developer relationship and to think differently about several of our legacy businesses. We are still a small company with limited resources, but now we have a focus on this important new technology and areas where we can be a first mover by utilizing it properly.
>
> So the third thing we did—creating this alliance with the software developer Liberty Software—came directly as a result of the e-strategy process. We now understand we've got a very significant

business opportunity here. We don't want to shift our focus 100 percent to the Internet, because we don't want to derail the transformation. But the process did help us better understand exactly what's going on out there. The one effect that was very, very important to us was that we decided to accelerate our discussions with Liberty Software and get our strategic partnership done, because they have a very significant piece of Web-enabled electronic document management software. And we are now their single largest value-added reseller in terms of geographic coverage and feet on the street.

We had been looking for about a year for not just *any* but the *right* EDMS software developer that we could align with. My guess is that if we had stayed on the trajectory we were on, it was going to be another six months before we would have come to closure. And we decided that was the one thing that could, at the same time, *not* defocus us but *create even more focus* to the transformation strategy and let the outside world know that we're serious about using emerging technologies to get critical information from paper to the desktop. We're right there. Liberty Software produces two products in electronic document management: a client server technology and very clearly Web-enabled ASP-type technology. And we made an alliance with them because we didn't want anyone else to have the single largest geographic coverage for them. We're their largest value-added reseller. They have other resellers, but nobody with our breadth, nobody with our scope in terms of feet on the street, and importantly, nobody with our strategy. It still is, in the end, a very unique strategy.

If you put those three seemingly independent events together, they very clearly demonstrate that we're serious about the TAB strategy. We are not going to be stuck with the legacy businesses just because they produce revenue. That's not what it's about. It's about getting focused. It's about driving on this know-how driving Force. And it's about using emerging technologies.

Another step in the e-strategy process had a galvanizing effect on Kantz and his team: the killer.com analysis. This exercise enables the team to envision a killer.com, which could rise up to put them out of business.

As Kantz recalls,

> We took it from the position, "Who's out there that could kill us off?" It had a very profound effect. I was on the killer.com team that was creating the strategy to confront TAB, and it was a real eye-opener. Here we were going through a transformation already, but one of the things we realized was that as important as the old legacy business was, it is now unimportant. And we must get out of it as quickly as we can. We must move aggressively to the new business model, because this is a drag on us. This is a drag on our resources. And it will continue to be in fact over the next year. If we don't act precipitously to move away from those legacy businesses, it will be a drag on exploiting these new technologies.

Looking back from just one year later, TAB is a company that has taken giant steps toward realizing a completely transformed organization with an innovative new business model. The implementation, as Kantz describes it, will take time, but TAB's people have recognized the necessity of mobilizing quickly to make it happen. "The killer.com concept is a great way of engaging people to think outside the day-to-day operations and actually think about the competitive risks that could face us in the future," says Kantz. "This process changes your perspective about how fast you need to move!"

CHAPTER

7

Demystifying The E-Nigma

In November 1999 Ken Bohlen showed up to begin his new position as chief information officer of Textron. As he told *The Wall Street Journal*, what greeted him on his first day was the discovery that there were 104 unrelated Web projects under way in various units of the company's 250 factories around the world. According to Bohlen, half were "vaporware" and the other half were "brochureware." None of them were going to generate much revenue or cut costs. Bohlen's observation: None of Textron's managers understood the Internet's capabilities or knew how to use the Internet to their advantage.

The Internet is a mystery to most executives, and any mystery is a challenge to a good problem solver. Since we at DPI consider ourselves problem solvers, some time ago we embarked on a journey to crack the e-nigma and make it understandable to laypeople.

THE E-NABLERS

The Internet e-nigma can be demystified only if one understands the Internet's *capabilities* and can rationally identify where and when the Internet will affect one's business model. We have found that the Internet has twelve basic capabilities, or *e-nablers*, that can be applied to any business:

- Aggregation
- Build to order
- Customer self-service
- Producer direct
- Channel integration
- Syndication
- Marketable knowledge
- Product rebundling
- Market exchanges
- Dynamic pricing
- Portals
- One-to-one marketing

Aggregation

Aggregation is the ability to recruit large groups of buyers and/or sellers in order to obtain better costs or prices. The Internet facilitates two forms of aggregation: *demand aggregation and supply aggregation.*

Demand aggregation could also be called demand collection. This is a key capability of the Internet which enables an organization to aggregate demand for a certain product or service and then use that increased volume to obtain better prices. A good example is Priceline.com, which originated the use of this e-nabler. The day Priceline.com went on-line, it removed the airlines' ability to price their product and placed it in the hands of consumers.

Priceline assembles large numbers of people who want to travel by air and then uses the accumulated volume to exert pressure on the airlines to come up with the cheapest price. And the model works! Over 200,000 people per week are using this service, and that number is growing at a 30 to 40 percent rate. Furthermore, Jay Walker, Priceline's founder, has a patent on this business model which will make it almost impossible for the airlines to respond in kind. One can expect Walker to extend this e-nabler to other product categories and cause havoc in each industry he chooses to infiltrate.

Two current examples of *supply aggregators* are Wal-Mart and Home Depot. These two companies do the opposite of what Priceline does. Instead of recruiting large numbers of consumers—demand—they recruit large numbers of vendors—supply—extract the lowest cost, and pass on the savings to their customers.

Build to Order

No company is better suited to find an Internet e-nabler that directly supports its business strategy than Dell Computer. The build-to-order e-nabler was made to order for Dell. This "e-nabler" does exactly what it says: It allows customers to place an order for a product configured to each customer's specific requirements. In fact, Dell should not be referred to as a "computer manufacturer" but rather as a "computer configurator," which is a better description of its business strategy.

Homegrocer.com is another company that exploits this capability. The use of this capability enables a customer to place an order for groceries on-line, configured to that customer's precise needs, just as a person would do by going to a store. In this case, the order is delivered the next day at a time specified by the customer and allows the customer to avoid the hassle of having to go to a crowded supermarket in the first place. Homegrocer also provides a host of other features, such the best choice of spices or vegetables to accompany the meat one has chosen as well as tips on how to prepare it. Imagine shopping from home with your own private chef giving you advice on the side.

Customer Self-Service

FedEx Custom Critical, formerly known as Roberts' Express and a DPI client, discovered this e-nabler during its use of our e-strategy process, which is described in a later chapter.

The company's business strategy is based on exploiting breakdowns in the just-in-time delivery system that is in place between companies and their suppliers. Whenever this system fails and the goods do not arrive on time, FedEx Custom Critical's strategy kicks in. That occurs when the company receives a call from a customer that finds itself in that predicament. FedEx Custom Critical has two thousand trucks strategically located around the country waiting for such a call. While on the phone with a dispatcher, using a sophisticated satellite system, the customer is guaranteed a specific time when the item will be picked up and delivered.

When management was introduced to the customer self-service e-nabler, it suddenly discovered that instead of going through a dispatcher, the customer could be given direct access to its fleet of trucks and, using the satellite system, locate the truck closest to the supplier's facility and contract with the truck operator directly, bypassing the dispatcher altogether. This is the way to exploit the Internet e-nabler called *customer self-service.*

Producer Direct

No single group of people is as concerned about the Internet as insurance agents, and justifiably. At the root of their concern is an e-nabler called *producer direct* The Internet provides a producer, or a manufacturer of a product or service, the opportunity to sell directly to the end user bypassing the traditional methods of selling and distributing through third-party agents, reps, or distributors.

This e-nabler is a death threat to all the intermediaries between a producer and a customer. This process is called *disintermediation* and is particularly prevalent in the area of intangible services such as insurance. Many CEOs of insurance companies are agonizing over this issue, and it is of strategic importance to the future of those firms. They are faced with the e-dilemma.

Do I or don't I bypass our brokers and sell direct? The CEO is damned if he does and damned if he doesn't. This e-dilemma is a classic Catch-22. If the CEO does this, she risks alienating the brokers and losing her only source of revenue. If she doesn't, she risks losing big chunks of revenue to a Dell-type competitor that might make the Internet its own strategy.

In the United Kingdom the Prudential Insurance Company has entered the banking industry by using this e-nabler. It has started an on-line bank through a Web site entitled egg.com. Since it wasn't in the banking business previously, it has no bricks and mortar branches as the established players do, and by using the Internet in this manner, it has changed the rules of play in its own favor.

Channel Integration

This e-nabler is the exact opposite of the one we just discussed. Instead of disintermediating the existing channels, this e-nabler attempts to *integrate* them with the Internet to create a coherent sales and distribution system that gives a company an additional competitive advantage.

Two companies currently deploying this e-nabler are Home Depot and The Gap. Home Depot has integrated the Internet with its stores and catalog. A customer can browse through the Home Depot catalog, select an item, order and pay for it on-line, and pick it up at the local store at a prearranged time. The Gap uses this e-nabler in a similar manner by integrating its catalog, stores, and advertising with the Internet. The whole system is seamless. A customer can buy on the Internet, take delivery through the postal service or United Parcel Service, discover that the item does not fit, and return it to any gap store for full credit.

Channel integration might be the e-nabler that can solve the "broker dilemma" faced by the insurance company CEOs mentioned above. Some forms of insurance which are self-explanatory, such a term insurance, probably can be sold over the Internet, while more complex forms which require consultation with an expert could continue to be handled through brokers and agents.

Syndication

Syndication enables a company to sell products or services to customers who then "package" them with other products that have been "syndicated" from other suppliers who, in turn resell or deliver the "package" to a third party.

Syndication, which is now available through the Internet, brings together three players, each with a different role. The first is the *originator*. This is the organization that creates the content, such as Disney with its continuous flow of animated film characters. Others are Charlie Schulz and Scott Adams, the "originators" of *Charlie Brown* and *Dilbert*, respectively.

The second player in this drama is the *syndicator*, which is the organization that buys the originator's content, combines it with content from other originators, and packages this content in a variety of formats to attract the third party in this play: the *distributor*. An example is a company called United Features, which purchases Schulz's and Adams's comic strips, packages them with others, and sells them to newspaper companies all over the world.

The *distributor* is the organization which interacts with customers. The distributor uses *syndication* as a method to reduce the cost of acquiring content. E-Trade is a good example of a distributor. E-Trade syndicates content from Reuters for news; Bridge Information for quotes; Big Charts for stock price graphics, and so forth.

The Internet accelerates the flow of information and thus the syndication of products by by dot-com companies.

Marketable Knowledge

Over the course of time, every organization accumulates large volumes of knowledge that relates to various parts of its business. In many instances that knowledge is stored and left to rot. The Internet provides a capability that enables a company to turn idle knowledge into a valuable asset by digitizing it and making it available on the Web.

One of our clients is Cancer Treatment Centers of America (CTCA). Its CEO, Dick Stephenson, is on a crusade to eradicate cancer from this planet. Over the years CTCA has accumulated vast quantities of information about various aspects of cancer that until recently lay dormant in one or another of its several facilities. Much of that information would be of great value to help educate new cancer patients about their disease. Medical professionals, such as doctors in training, would also be interested in having access to this information.

CTCA has done just that. It has created a Web site that is organized by cancer category and makes available, for free, all the treatment options, both traditional and holistic, to help patients make more informed decisions.

Every organization has a bank of experiential data that could be packaged in a variety of different forms, and sold on the Internet to create brand-new revenue streams for an organization.

Product Rebundling

Cendant Corporation is a conglomerate which owns hotel chains, car rental companies, travel agency chains, and a real estate franchisor called Century 21. Until recently, these businesses all were operated separately, although it was always the CEO's strategy to combine their product offerings in some manner. Unfortunately, he did not have a mechanism to make that occur, and the synergy that he was seeking did not materialize, that is, until the Internet arrived.

This e-nabler, which is called *product rebundling*, allows an entity to use the Internet to bundle closely related but separate and different products or services in combinations that would not be possible on a stand-alone basis. The new e-commerce entity adds value in a manner that the separate organizations cannot.

A good friend of ours is in the process of setting up an Internet company whose strategy is based totally on exploiting this e-nabler. The concept is brilliant. The company has negotiated agreements with the major universities and book publishers for the right to reproduce digitally all their "knowledge" manuscripts. The company will resell the content of those publications in whole or in part, which will then be downloaded from the Internet. In fact, you will be able to order Chapters 2 and 6 from one book and Chapters 3 and 8 from another book and, 15 minutes later, pick it up, nicely bound, at the local photocopier.

Market Exchanges

This e-nabler is the opposite of demand aggregation. In this case, it is the *producers* who aggregate *production* volumes in an industry in order to let *customers* know *how much* product is available and *where*. In some industries the *market exchange* e-nabler allows interested customers to *bid* on the inventory that is available.

Two current examples of this e-nabler at work are Plasticsnet .com and Metalsite.com. Both are sponsored by several producers in that industry which publish their inventory and then hold on-line auctions. These exchanges provide a more cost-efficient method to get products to markets. Market exchanges exist in many industries and are probably the most popular of the twelve e-nablers.

Dynamic Pricing

This e-nabler takes market exchanges a step farther. As the word *dynamic* implies, products offered through this e-nabler have dynamic or even volatile prices. In accordance with the classic law of supply and demand, the price varies with each transaction, depending on the balance between demand and supply. Sometimes the producer wins; sometimes the customer wins.

One company that is currently testing this e-nabler is Budget Rent-a-Car, which allows a customer to make an offer on what he or she is willing to pay depending on how many cars are on the lot at any time of the day. Budget then accepts or rejects that offer on the basis of that number. As a result, the price is "dynamic" in that it can differ with every transaction.

Portals

A *portal* is a Web capability developed by an organization in which a company offers its own products as well as products from competitors. The company does this so that it will be perceived as an "objective" party to the buying process. It hopes that this "objectivity" will bring it a fair share of the sales generated.

One company that uses this e-nabler is an insurance company called Progressive located in Cleveland. Its Web site is a "portal" to its own insurance products as well as some from its competitors.

Progressive gladly "refers" prospects to its lower-priced competitors because its proprietary software is designed to weed out potentially unprofitable customers up front.

Sometimes competitors come together to construct a portal site that will give potential customers an overview of products that can be purchased separately from each company. One of our clients, the Pulte Corporation, has collaborated with its three most significant competitors in the home-building industry—Centex, Kaufmann & Broad, and Lennar—to use this e-nabler. The four companies include all their models and locations to allow the customer to do some "preshopping" before driving out to visit the real thing.

One-to-One Marketing

The other day, while reading my favorite weekly sports magazine, I turned to page 67 to discover the following message:

> Michel Robert
> Are you considering refinancing your home mortgage? If you are, please call us for a better rate.
>
> ABC Bank

So surprised was I to see my name in print that I read the rest of the advertisement, something I never do. This is called *one-to-one marketing.* Electronic technology allows companies to construct databases that can store enormous amounts of information that can be used to zero in on a prospect with a clearly defined profile, one-to-one. The Internet allows this to happen on a PC rather than in a magazine. This technique is called *narrowcasting* as opposed to *broadcasting,* which is targeted at a broad audience, and it will be the method of choice for marketing in the future.

THE E-NABLER: UNLEASHING INTERNET INNOVATION

Once your people understand these 12 e-nablers, they will be able to think of many ways in which these capabilities can be exploited across the business. The issue now is to ensure that these Internet e-nablers are deployed in a manner that supports the *business strategy* of the enterprise.

GOOD NEWS/BAD NEWS

The bad news associated with your newly acquired knowledge of the Internet's 12 capabilities is that if you decide to use them to create a new business model to deploy your business strategy, you will have to make significant investments in IT systems. As was noted earlier, in view of the high failure rate, you are entering a *high-risk* game.

The good news is that you can substantially reduce that risk by being the *architect* of your e-strategy, a role most CEOs today are abdicating.

Framing an e-Strategy

Interview:
Mark O'Brien,
President and COO,
Pulte Corporation

It may be possible to build a house without a blueprint, especially for an experienced builder who has built a similar structure before. This builder knows what it will look like, what materials to use, what it's likely to cost, and what kinds of problems he or she may run into. While this can be done, it's certainly not the most intelligent way to build a house. Unfortunately, a lot of companies have tried to do the same thing with their Internet initiatives, with disastrous results: cost overruns, overlapping applications, and projects that seem to go on endlessly. The fundamental difference between the house and the Internet is that there are no proven Internet models for the business. No one's ever built one like it before. No one knows what it should look like, how long it will take, what problems will be encountered, what it will cost, and most important, whether it will do what's needed to support the business strategy.

Pulte Corporation had been involved in the Internet over the past three-plus years, implementing a reasonably well-developed plan. Yet early in 2000, the people at Pulte—a major national home builder that *does* use blueprints to build houses—saw that the time had come to design a comprehensive blueprint for an Internet strategy that would fully support its *business* strategy.

But let's step back a bit in time to see how it arrived at that conclusion.

Building the Business Strategy

In the mid-1990s Pulte Corporation set out to "change the rules of play in the home-building market," as CEO Bob Burgess then stated. Through DPI's strategic thinking process, the $2 billion company made a commitment to several ambitious goals, including doubling the size of the company by the year 2000, which it has successfully accomplished.

The guiding mantra through the ensuing years of extraordinary growth has always been "delight the customer." Most people who have been through the process of building a home know that the experience can be fraught with delays, blown budgets, and disappearing contractors. It can be anything but delightful. Pulte was determined to change all that.

First, it trimmed down the company by shedding businesses unrelated to home building. Pulte got down to a solid foundation: its home-building and home mortgage businesses. Then it worked to apply more sophisticated marketing techniques to understand its customers and markets and focused on delivering the highest-quality home possible. This work evolved into a strategy Pulte calls Homeowner for Life, which seeks to extend the strong customer relationship Pulte develops over the course of building a customer's new home. The ultimate goal of Homeowner for Life is to sell additional products and services by maintaining that customer relationship long after the house sale is complete. These concepts required the integration of skills not always found in home building: market research, consumer marketing, and an obsession with quality improvement throughout the complex value chain and sales process. Pulte's exceptional growth in sales and profits and consistently high customer satisfaction marks attest to the success of its strategy.

Enter the Internet

In the middle of all this change, Pulte, as early as 1995, recognized the emergence of technology as an important tool to improve and grow the business. In its embrace of technology, it was ahead of many companies in the home-building industry. This trend continued as Pulte was an early adopter of the Internet to support its business operations. As technology and the Internet became an increasingly important part of the business, the company felt the need for a cohesive overall strategy and opted for DPI's e-strategy process to create it.

As the president and Chief Operating Officer (COO) Mark O'Brien, recalls,

> We began to develop a long-range e-business plan that would help guide us for the foreseeable future. As part of this process, we formed an e-business team to develop a more comprehensive Internet strategy. The preliminary work of this group provided a pretty solid foundation that we brought into the process. The process helped us define and validate the strategy and prioritize some of the underlying tactics. That's the junction in the road we found ourselves in. Seven or eight years ago, Mike Robert and his team assisted us in developing a strategic plan. That experience was positive, and we thought Mike could provide some of the same assistance in developing our e-strategy. By coincidence, they had just developed a process to help companies formulate an e-strategy.
>
> Pulte had already developed a number of e-business initiatives focused on capturing B2C and B2B business opportunities. We had established an e-business team reporting directly to senior management, guiding and implementing our process. We really saw the

> process as a tool to help us focus and prioritize Internet-related activities that are designed to support Pulte's core home-building business.

People from a wide array of disciplines within Pulte were assembled to hammer out the new e-strategy. One of the most critical steps in the process is to bring the group to a common understanding of the Internet's potential effects. To accomplish this, DPI has developed a set of 12 e-nablers which represent the Internet's basic business models. These e-nablers demystify the Internet for businesspeople by identifying specific capabilities of the Internet that can be used to leverage a company's key strengths.

Says O'Brien:

> Understanding of the Internet varied widely. We assembled a group of about 60 people to go through this process. Some had great knowledge of the Internet and e-business, while others are more focused on our traditional home-building activities and thus less exposed and conversant with the powers of e-commerce.
>
> The e-nabler framework is a great way to present a complex series of concepts. I know the participants in our group who were unfamiliar with Internet-based business models found that the information helped focus their thoughts and ideas as we advanced through the subsequent stages of the process.

Once the e-nablers were understood, the core business and information processes that tie the company together were mapped in detail. The process then allowed the work teams to identify the points of impact where these different e-nablers may affect these processes both positively and negatively.

A list of specific potential Internet applications was developed that would leverage the positive impacts and mitigate the negative ones. Those applications were filtered for strategic fit, cost, benefits, and ease of implementation. The resulting short list was deemed to include the applications most crucial to supporting the business strategy.

As O'Brien comments,

> One of the interesting results, having gone through the e-strategy process, was that each of the teams came up with applications working independently which had a lot of common characteristics. There were several overlaps and links between one and another. As we developed our Internet blueprint, we were able to merge all of our various disciplines and visions into a real value chain of e-commerce.
>
> We are in the very final stages of a comprehensive Internet blueprint that will address all aspects of our home-building value chain from managing the customer experience to efficiently linking our contractors, vendors, and suppliers. We're now working to set priorities and establish the teams that will drive the implementation as we go forward.
>
> I don't think there's any question that as a result of going through the e-strategy process, we eliminated some applications from our previously articulated strategy, added some others, and in fact identified a lot of enhancements that will have value. Fully implementing this program will take place over a period of months and maybe years, but at least we're beginning with the end in mind.
>
> Having gone through the strategic thinking process seven years ago and having arrived at a clear strategic direction for the company and now exploiting the e-nablers together with our strengths and understanding the competitive environment that we were in, there is every reason to believe that we will get the same positive result from our e-business strategy that we got for our corporate strategy.

A Look at E-Competition

The process then gave Pulte an opportunity to look at the Internet from its competitors' perspective. The competitor.com team used the process to determine how competitors might use the Internet:

> The competitor team did a great job of providing insight into where the industry is likely to head and how specific competitors might respond to our various initiatives at Pulte. Working independently of the rest of the teams, I think the competitor team validated many of the strategic initiatives that we are considering, while at the same time highlighting some of the opportunities and risks inherent in our approach. Overall, I think it was a very valuable contributor to the process and a necessary one.

In a similar vein, the killer.com team was given the assignment of designing a new e-competitor whose purpose would be to invalidate Pulte's business model and possibly put Pulte out of business. What form would it take? How vulnerable would Pulte be? What could the company do to mitigate such a threat?

Although he understandably provides no specifics, O'Brien says simply, "With respect to the killer.com team, they did some very interesting work. I think as the result of their work, we are incorporating some features into our strategy that will insulate us from the killer. We have a vision of that killer.com, but I don't think we got absolute clarity because that killer may manifest itself in varying ways over the years to come. But I think we have an idea where it would come from and what we might do about it."

Indeed, the flexibility of DPI's strategic thinking process and e-strategy process may be what gives these processes strength and longevity within an organization. As they become part of the fabric of the company's thinking, they provide a basis for continuous reevaluation as the world changes. This is particularly crucial with the Internet, since the future is filled with unknown developments.

Says O'Brien, "On the other hand, I think there are some knowns. The Internet has touched every one of us. It is changing the way we live on a daily basis. I don't think there is any question that it is changing the home-building landscape, as it is many other businesses. I think we just need to be prepared to develop with it. We're obviously excited about the future. I think the process we've been through added clarity to our e-strategy. As we go forward, we will continue to apply many of the tools that are in the kit to the varying opportunities that the e-commerce world present to us."

Perhaps the most important result is that Pulte now has an agreed-upon e-strategy that fully supports its business strategy, which has proved to be successful throughout the last decade.

O'Brien states:

> Our vision is to effectively link the entire home-building value chain from customers to contractors and suppliers. We recognize that this is an ambitious undertaking. It will require an enormous investment of people and financial resources. The process helped us be more specific and precise about the potential benefits associated with these various programs as well how best to prioritize the initiatives.
>
> Pulte Corporation is a home builder. We will continue to focus on our core home-building business, delighting our customers with every house we build and the entire home buying, building, and ownership experience. E-business is not a separate activity. It needs to add value—must add value, in fact—and be integrated into our day-to-day operations and support our core home-building and

mortgage businesses. It's the function of technology to support and enhance communications with our customers and our business partners before, during, and after a home is built. And I think the e-strategy process helps ensure that we will retain that focus.

CHAPTER

8

The Critical Gap: No e-Strategy Architect

One of the major inconveniences associated with the desire to join the Internet club is the need for a major investment in IT systems. Unfortunately, you are entering a *high-cost/high-risk* arena.

This is best illustrated by a study done by the Standish Group of the success and failure rates of IT projects. The results were as follows:

Eighty-four percent of IT projects are late, over budget, or canceled.

The cost to U.S. corporations is over $184 billion per year.

Completed projects achieve only 60 percent of their objectives.

Consider the following examples. After several years of attempting to install an SAP system without success, Waste Management finally conceded defeat, wrote off its investment of $230 million, and decided to go back to square one. The Bank of

America, as it was then known, did the same thing when it wrote off its multimillion-dollar investment in implementing a software program called Masternet that was intended to manage complex stock and real estate portfolios for large institutions. After the project ran $60 million over budget and was 27 months late, the CEO finally pulled the cord and aborted it.

What is at the root of *all* these failures? To us the answer is very simple. To make the transformation from a conventional business model to an e-business model highly dependent on the use of the Internet, one must understand *how IT systems are developed.* Unfortunately, to most CEOs this is foreign terrain, and this key area of resource allocation is delegated to a task force of some kind with a mandate to develop a miracle plan.

THE IT SYSTEM DEVELOPMENT PROCESS

IT systems consist of hardware and software. Basically, an IT system uses software that runs on hardware, as shown in the graphic below.

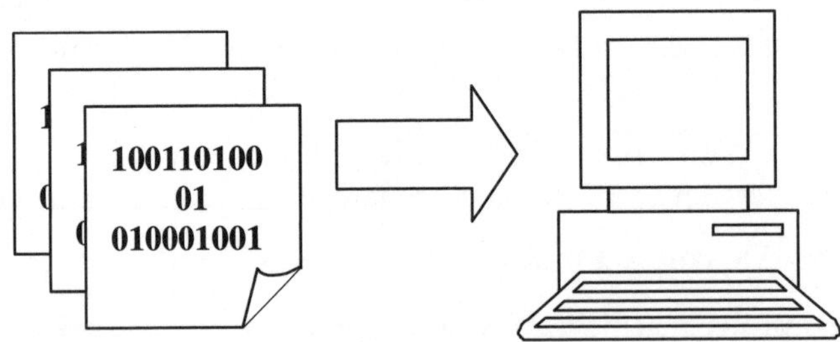

To ensure that the hardware and the software work in harmony, someone has to design the software so that it is compatible with the hardware (see the following graphic).

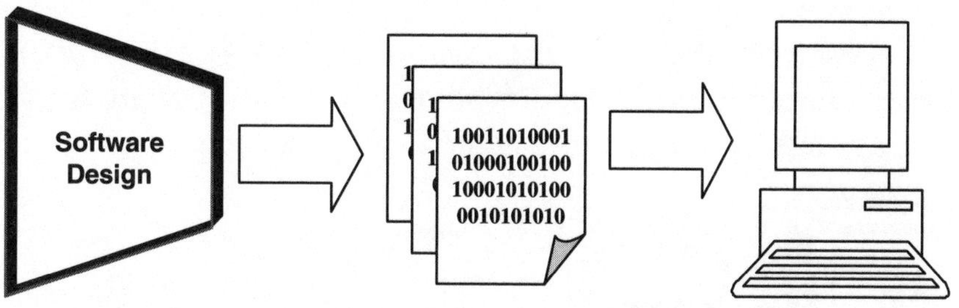

Furthermore, in most companies these steps are done by an outside "system integrator." The system integrator designs or buys the software and decides on which hardware it will run. The following graphic illustrates how all IT vendors fit into these three parts of the process.

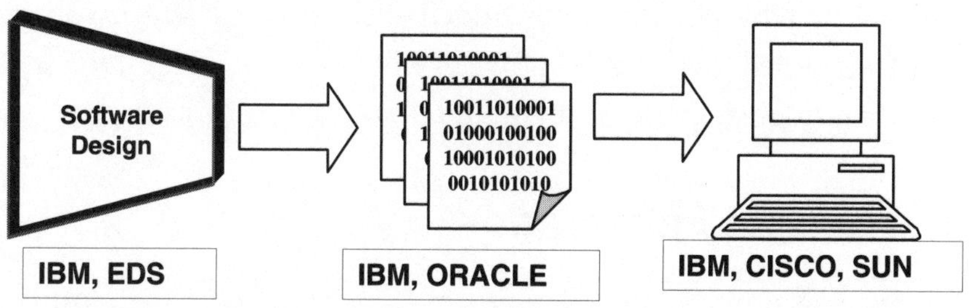

This is the process used by all system integrators to provide a "solution" to a request for IT assistance. However, for a company to transform itself from its traditional business model to an e-business model, some additional steps must be included upstream, as is shown in the graphic below.

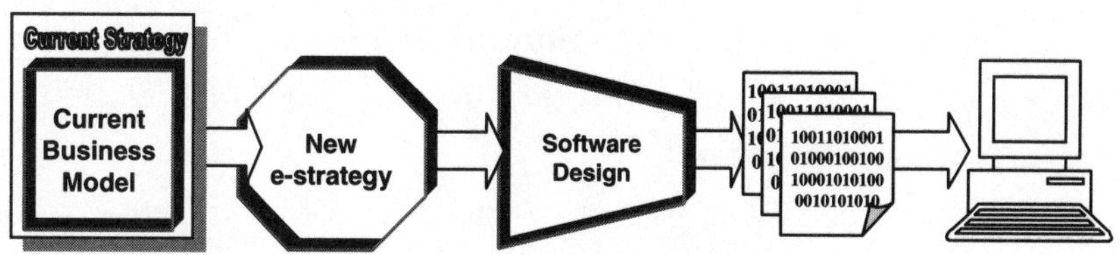

In our view, there is a major *gap* in this process. Who designs the e-strategy which will determine the most appropriate e-business model required to migrate to the new economy?

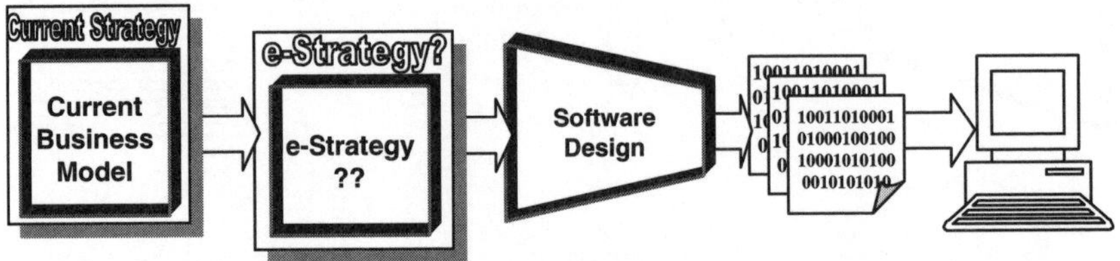

The answer today is simple: the outside consultant. In other words, the so-called Internet consultant becomes the *architect* of the client's Internet strategy. Two recent studies, one by McKinsey and another by Forrester, concluded that lack of client involvement which led to a lack of knowledge of the client's requirements was the principal cause of the high failure rate of IT projects.

THE ABSENT ARCHITECT

"As the world moves to global networks, we aim to be the plumbers with our optics, silicon, software and services," said Richard McGinn, the CEO of Lucent Technology, to *Forbes* magazine. Marc Andreessen, the creator of the Netscape browser and now the CEO of the start-up Loudcloud, describes his new company as one that "assembles the plumbing that's needed to run a busy Web site—everything from server computers to database software."[1]

Both of these CEOs have quite accurately described their role as the "plumbers" of Internet solutions. Unfortunately, in many companies the plumber has become the architect of the client's Internet strategy by default.

Because most CEOs and most members of management do not understand how the Internet works, they cannot articulate

[1]Neil Weinberg and Nikhil Hutheesing, "Wired and Restless," *Business Week*, February 7, 2000, p. 91.

how they could use the Internet to benefit the company. In other words, they do not have a *coherent Internet strategy* together with a *blueprint* of the *business requirements* the Internet should fulfill.

In the strategic thinking process, the CEO is the owner of the process and the architect of the strategy that results. In regard to the Internet, however, CEOs withdraw from the process, put the design of an Internet strategy in the hands of an outside consultant, and abdicate their right to be the architect of their own Internet strategies. They in fact put their Internet "destiny" in the hands of the plumber—the outside IT consultant. The plumber becomes the de facto architect, with the result that the company ends up with a lot of pipes. In many cases the client ends up with a system that is designed to suit the capabilities of the consultant rather than the requirements of the client.

In defense of the plumbers of the consulting world, however, it is only fair to say that this situation is not the position they like to be in. The major difficulty IT consultants encounter, and all of them will tell you this very loudly, is that most of their clients *cannot articulate their requirements.* They will also tell you that they would rather not be the architect and that the client should be his or her own architect. Knowing that the client probably will not be able to articulate his or her requirements, they insert into their proposal an amount equal to 15 to 20 percent of the project fee for flushing out the customer's requirements. And even then, they will tell you that the requirements they are able to extract are still vague and incomplete. In fact, industry experts will tell you that the high failure rate of IT projects is caused primarily by *unclear or ambiguous client requirements.*

Thus the first dichotomy: The client abdicates his role as architect because of a lack of understanding of the Internet, and the IT consultant finds herself in an undesired role by default. The client is then not satisfied with the solution, and the consultant is frustrated with the client's inability to articulate "what they want" the Internet to do. And around and around we go.

Then comes the second dichotomy: The client looks for outside help only to discover that traditional consultants such as McKinsey and Bain don't understand the Internet and the new e-business consultants don't understand the client's industry.

In another study conducted by Forrester Research, the following statements were made by companies that sought help from both types.

About the management consultants:

> We considered management consultants but felt they are too traditional in their thinking. Instead of giving us action items for the Internet, they were still talking about how companies operate in existing markets.[2]
>
> We recently met with one of the larger management consulting firms, and it was obvious that their consultants did not know much about the Web.[3]

About the e-business integrators:

> Retail banking is complicated, and we don't want flippant answers. In the end, our e-commerce integrator was not smart enough about our business, and a two-month project took four.[4]
>
> We hired Viant for a 90-day, fixed-price job. We ran into the problem of having to explain to them the peculiarities of our business.[5]

Our conclusion: *Never let the plumber be the architect of your Internet strategy!*

[2]Christine Spivey Overby, "eBusiness Strategy Needs Help," *The Forrester Report*, February 2000, pp. 4-5.
[3]Ibid.
[4]Ibid.
[5]Ibid.

THE DPI GOAL: THE CLIENT IS THE ARCHITECT

The goal of our process is to make life easier for both parties by making the *client the architect of the company's Internet strategy.* Our approach is based on three tenets we have learned from our work with over 400 companies that have used our strategic thinking process to formulate and deploy a business strategy successfully:

- Every company interacts with its customers in its own particular way, depending on the distinctiveness of its *business* strategy.
- No one understands the genetic code of the company better than do its employees
- The modus operandi on how to use the Internet as another tool to deploy a business strategy needs to be proprietary to each company and, as such, can be designed only by a company's own people.

With these three tenets in mind, we have developed an e-strategy process that produces the following outcome:

A unique blueprint of a new business model that leverages the Internet as a strategic weapon to cause commercial transactions to occur.

To achieve this outcome and make the client the architect of the Internet strategy, the client must have access to a *structured process* such as the one described later in this book.

Delivering a Clear Internet Strategy

Interview:
Bruce Simpson,
CEO,
Fedex Custom Critical

The Internet. Five years ago it was little more than a technical curiosity, a minor blip on the radar screens of most CEOs. Today, the Internet is everywhere. The financial pages are filled with tales of the latest dot-coms and their stratospheric market valuations.

But the real story of the Internet concerns the many thousands of established, conventional companies for which this truly revolutionary new technology has suddenly become one of the most pressing and perplexing issues ever faced.

Vexing new questions confront today's CEO. Where does the Internet fit in our industry? What new opportunities can we jump on? Where are the hidden threats? How can we prevent new e-competitors from infringing on our markets? How do we create an e-strategy that supports and even turbocharges our business strategy?

The management at FedEx Custom Critical, a FEDEX Corporation subsidiary (formerly Roberts Express), was grappling with questions like these when CEO Bruce Simpson decided to use DPI's new e-strategy process to enable his management team to chart a clear course through the Internet maze. A veteran of the strategic thinking process, he was a believer in the ability of these critical thinking tools to empower managers to reason through complex questions and take ownership of the conclusions.

e-Strategy: Where the Rubber Meets the Information Superhighway

FedEx Custom Critical is by no means a babe in the woods when it comes to sophisticated communications technology. A leader in the field of "expedited delivery," it employs over 2,000 trucks as well as air charter services that provide time-sensitive delivery of cargo of any size and weight anywhere, guaranteed within 15 minutes on pickup and delivery. All this is made possible by a proprietary system of satellite communications that can instantaneously locate any one of its trucks within 300 yards. Indeed, this communications capability was discovered to be the driving force of its strategy when FedEx Custom Critical went through the strategic thinking process a few years ago, as this driving force statement clearly shows:

> We provide dedicated transportation services that apply our superior, integrated communication network and controlled delivery system. We concentrate on customers with precise, time-critical needs in geographic areas with an adequate infrastructure and a critical mass of manufacturers and shippers. Our intent is to be the unsurpassed leader in measured customer satisfaction.

However, as advanced as FedEx Custom Critical was technologically, it had not yet developed a cohesive overall *Internet* strategy for the enterprise. Says Bruce Simpson of its Internet initiatives,

> Our involvement had been limited, sporadic. We talked about the ability to trace shipments through the Internet. We asked customers themselves, in our monthly satisfaction survey, to what extent they were using the Internet for connectivity with their suppliers and

> carriers. So we had developed very specific connectivity with customers, tracing shipments. But from the standpoint of falling back from the trees and looking at the forest, we didn't have any idea of how we wanted to integrate, for the long term, the Internet into our business strategy, into the future of how we're going to grow and differentiate the business.

Joe Greulich, the director of technology, concurs:

> The way it had worked was that our marketing people would prioritize Internet functions, but they had limited resources available to them. Our approach was very customer-focused, and it still is. We offered, for instance, brochureware on the web. We also offered the ability to trace or map a shipment. But as we go forward and offer more capabilities to our customers, we don't want to make our customers adapt to *our* system. We have a very structured way of doing business. In fact, it's one of our key strengths: our system for pickups and deliveries and tracking them. But we want to adapt ourselves to the way our customers do business, not the other way around. To make sure this stayed a customer-focused system, we had to either erase what we knew or just take a new approach. We realized that we were going to have to step up the investment we were making in the Internet and we needed a game plan.

A few months ago, the top 40 people in FedEx Custom Critical's management made a quantum jump forward in their thinking regarding e-business. Using the e-strategy process, the team embarked on the creation of an Internet strategy that fully supports the business strategy and places their resources where they will deliver the greatest benefit to their customers, truck drivers, and employees.

This e-strategy process is a codified set of steps that first of all "demystifies" the Internet. To do this, the Internet is broken down into 12 e-nablers that represent the basic capabilities of the Internet.

Says Greulich of these e-nablers, "You could feel them, but you wouldn't have been able to clearly identify them. And the fact that we could now identify them made the e-strategy process and the Internet very concrete and real. So it was very, very helpful, particularly for the less technical people in our organization. It wasn't a matter so much of catching up as of catching *on*."

During the e-strategy process the participants applied these e-nablers to a detailed mapping of all the core information processes inside and outside the company, determining where each e-nabler might affect the business positively or negatively.

As Joe Greulich sees it,

> The e-strategy process itself drives you to think about what information processes you have in place today, how your functions relate to each other and to your suppliers and customers. That exercise alone is a good thing to do. Then, added to that, is the *e-effect*, or the impact that the Internet will have on those things. That was, for us, a very educating thing to have happen. We have a better companywide understanding of all the information processes that are going on and the points of impact where the Internet can infringe on them.
>
> If you were to do that piecemeal, which is the traditional way for companies to go about this, it would take years to get that kind of understanding communicated across the company. The bigger the company, the longer it takes. We compressed a lot of communication through this process.

With the company's business strategy and driving force used as a filter, the points of impact were prioritized on the basis their relative benefit for or threat to the company. From that analysis, concepts for specific e-business applications were developed to address those opportunities or threats. Applications with the top priority then were analyzed to create a detailed list of "musts and wants" for each planned initiative. The result is that FedEx Custom Critical now has a prioritized set of e-projects, each with a defined set of business requirements for the hardware and software solution developers to follow. This is in effect a unique blueprint for a new business model designed to leverage the Internet as a strategic weapon that will cause transactions to happen. More important, *the company's management* designed this blueprint, specifically to strengthen the company's driving force and business strategy.

As Greulich explains:

> The way we've looked at it is we're building a bridge from two sides of the river. On one side of the river is our business strategy: what do we do to keep going. And on the other side we're now building a bridge back from our Internet or e-strategy. And the real mission of execution is to make sure they meet in the middle so you can drive across it. We think we've got everybody on the bridge. We knew we *had* to merge the business strategy and the e-strategy together. In order to make that happen—that's a people thing—you've got to educate people. What I've found is that *acquiring* technology can always be done. *Applying* technology is really limited by how well people understand it, relate to it, and change with it. So you have to precede change with education. And that's really what this e-strategy process did for us. It educated us and guided us along on how to make these changes and how to start taking steps to make them happen. It was very clear to us that the e-strategy and the business strategy had to be linked. And we believe we've done that. Instead of me trying to dream up what's down the road and what's possible, our managers are doing it, and they're putting it into their

> business plans. We're getting ready to launch the business plan for next year incorporating the e-strategy. Where the long-term strategy meets your yearly budget is where the rubber meets the road. I've started to see those linkages happen. This overall education of the management team and the commitment of the management team are the best results of the e-strategy process.

Today FedEx Custom Critical has a solid foundation for its evolving e-strategy. From the CEO's chair, the most crucial aspect of that plan is this linkage between FedEx Custom Critical's business strategy, driving force, and e-strategy. Says Simpson:

> I'm sitting here right now with a list on my desk of the top two priorities together with the "musts and wants" and the measurements. We are in the process of determining the steps in getting these things done—the time line, the costs. We now have the means to determine what ongoing IT projects to shift resources from because we're going to have to say, "If this is the priority for the company, we're going to have to take resources from one place and move them to another." We all understand that the driving force is the capability of our information system, which we determined three years ago. Using that as a filter, we've been able to prioritize the list that came out of the e-strategy session, applying this new Internet connectivity to our customers, our drivers, and our people. And it's a beautiful combination because it has allowed us to take the information system and broaden it beyond even our current comprehension. Through the combination of the strategic thinking process and now the e-strategy process we're able to exploit the Internet to enhance our driving force. I love the idea that we can be linked to customers and offer them our service better than ever before. That has a real, viable linkage and potential for us.
>
> I guess I've been persuaded that with the dynamics and

magnitude of the changes taking place, whether you're in manufacturing or services, this is going to be the most powerful thing that's happened in the business world in this century or the last one. It's going to change everything about how we conduct our affairs with all of our resources, customers, and constituencies.

CHAPTER 9

The Second Imperative: Constructing the e-Strategy Blueprint

Every commercial organization exists to convert *resources* into products or services that satisfy the needs of *markets*. This concept is illustrated in the following graphic:

To accomplish this, every organization conducts a number of the following activities.

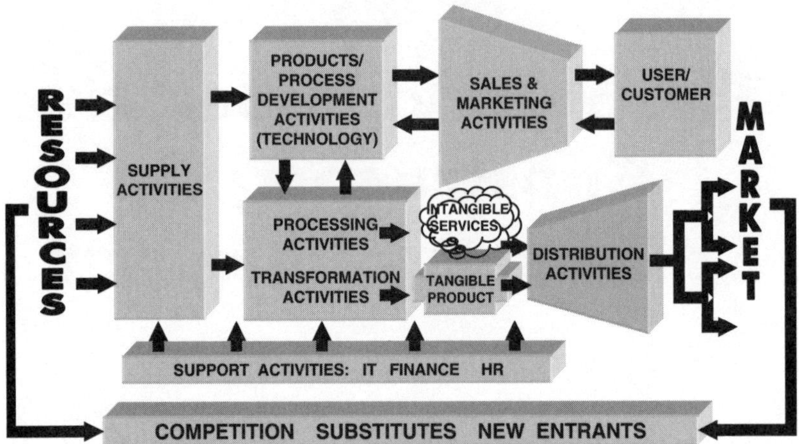

These are the activities that have become universal in nature and have evolved into separate *functions.* The key element of success is to ensure that these separate functions operate as an efficient and cohesive entity, not as disparate and independent "silos" going in different directions.

There are two elements that will achieve this togetherness:

- Cohesiveness is achieved by having a *clear business strategy* in place that everyone understands and is committed to; this strategy results from the strategic thinking process.
- Efficiency is dependent on how well these functions are "connected," which brings us to the key topic of this chapter: *information.*

INFORMATION: THE LIFEBLOOD OF INTERCONNECTIVITY

In most organizations, the highest costs are not those associated with materials or labor but the intangible and unseen costs associated with the inefficient *flow of information* from one function to another. This is the cost of retrieving, capturing, storing, and processing information along this chain of functions. In some industries, such as health care, banking, insurance, and retailing, these costs can represent over half of the cost of doing business.

Information is the link that keeps different functions *connected* to each other. It is the flow of such information across functions that determines the efficiency of an organization.

The activities of any single function are activated by a piece of information transmitted by a preceding function. Once the receiving function completes its activity, it sends information to the next function, which activates the next activity. For example, the sales function sends a sales forecast to the production function, which sets machinery into motion to make a specific quantity of products. Once these products are completed, the production function sends a piece of information to the distribution function to inform it to come and take the finished product and place it in the warehouse. And the chain repeats itself from one function to the other, as is shown in the following graphic.

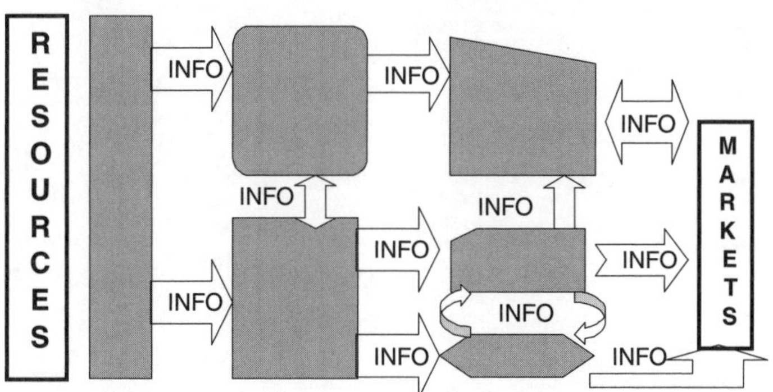

Information: The Lifeblood of an Organization

DISRUPTING INTERCONNECTIVITY

Every organization becomes dependent on the flow of information across functions, and it is in these areas of *interconnectivity* that the Internet has its most disruptive effect. The Internet is basically a *transporter of information.* However, because it can make more information available to more people more rapidly than can any other medium, the Internet has changed the rules of play in terms of how information gets transferred across functions. Unfortunately, most executives are not knowledgeable about what information flows across the organization and how it does this. The reason is simple: Until the advent of the Internet, there was no need to know.

Today, however, the CEO and the executive team *must* understand the flow of information in the organization because this is where the game will be won or lost in the future. To understand this flow and be able to act on it requires a *process,* something most organizations do not have in place.

THE DPI E-STRATEGY PROCESS

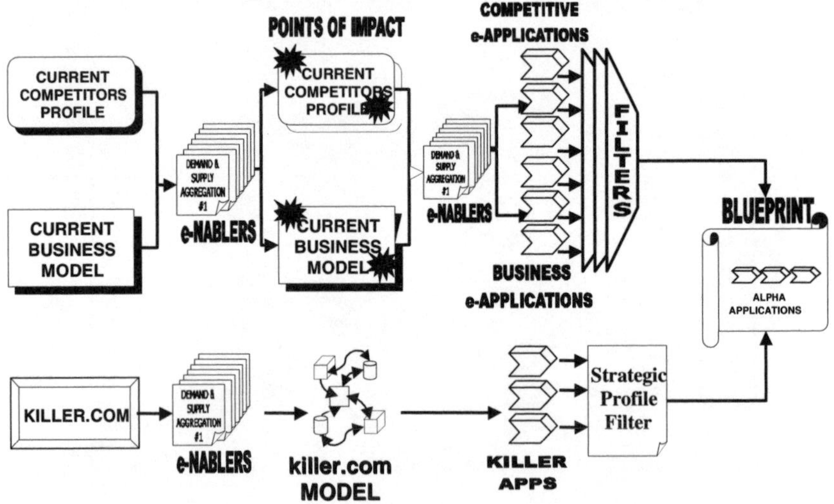

The process we have developed, tested, and validated with several clients has the following steps.

Step 1: Mapping the Organization's Lifeblood

To map the organization's lifeblood, the first step is to map out the flow of information through the organization's key operating functions and clearly identify the pieces of data that trigger each function's key activities. Together with both the *source* and the *recipient* of a particular piece of information.

We start by analyzing the current business model into its various functions, as shown in the following graphic.

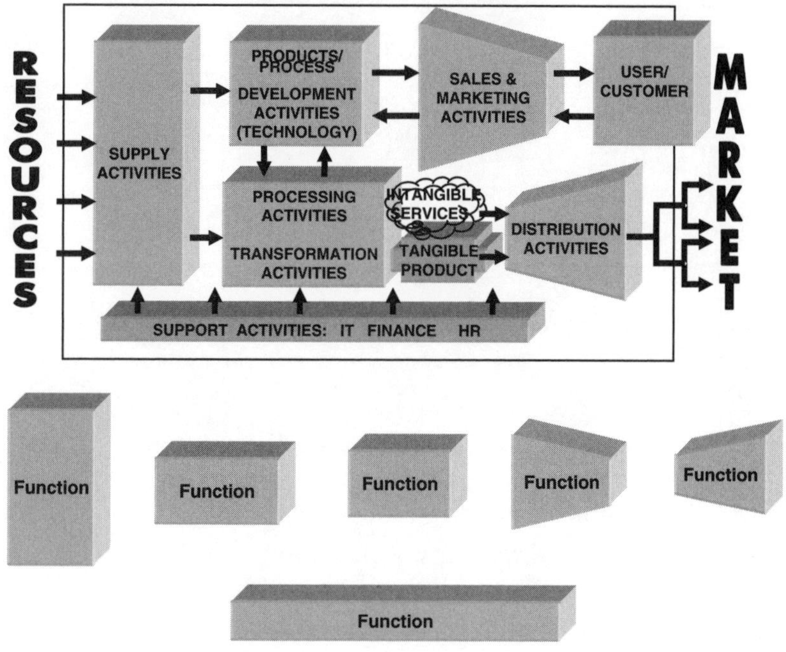

We then take each function and the major activities conducted there, together with the *input* utilized and the *output* generated.

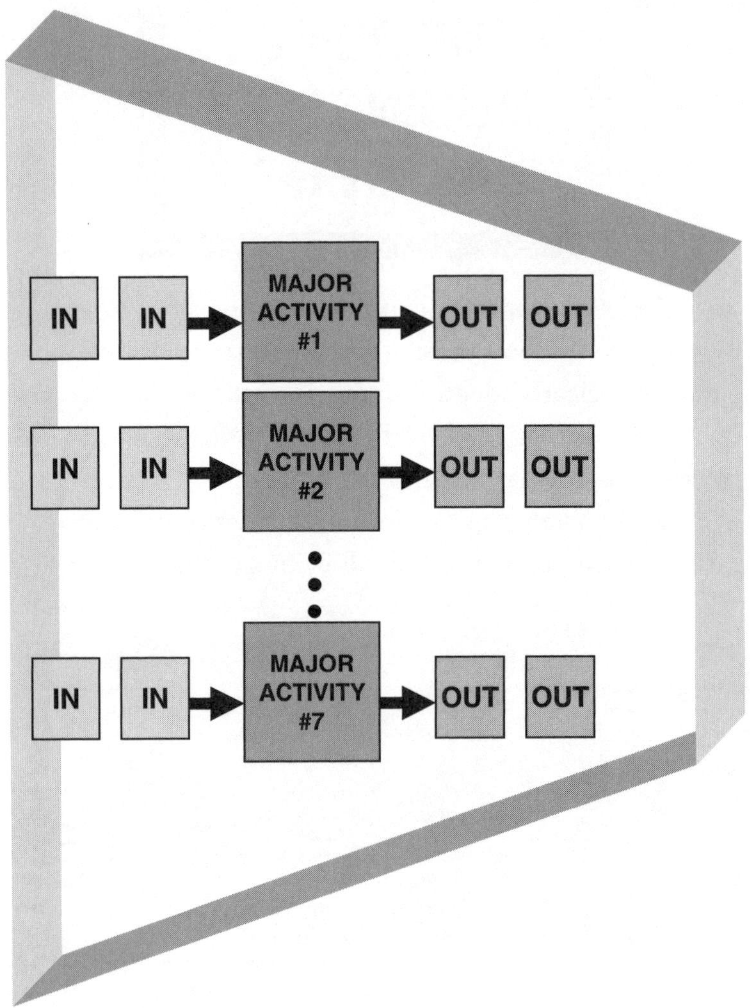

We then do this for all functions of the company and track the interconnectivity of those inputs and outputs. What we have now re-created is the information flow patterns, or genetic code, of the organization.

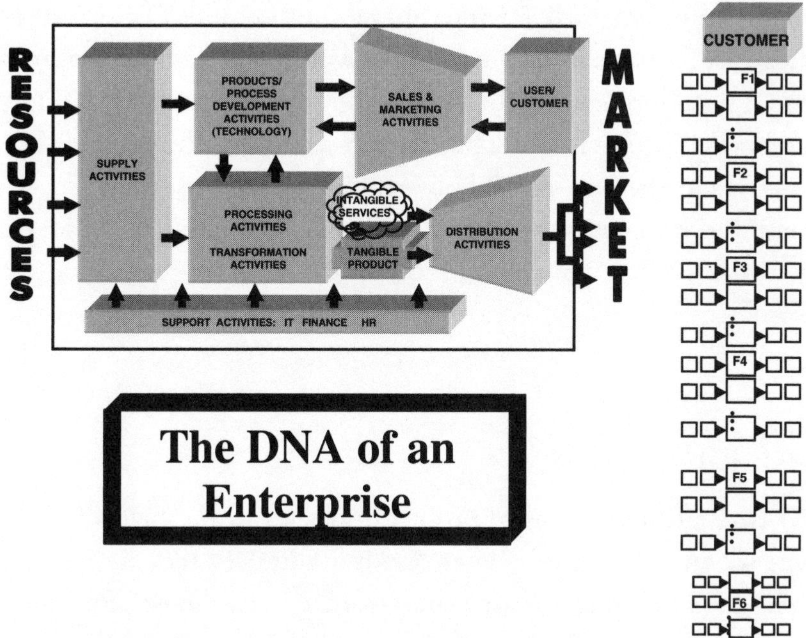

Step 2: Points of Impact

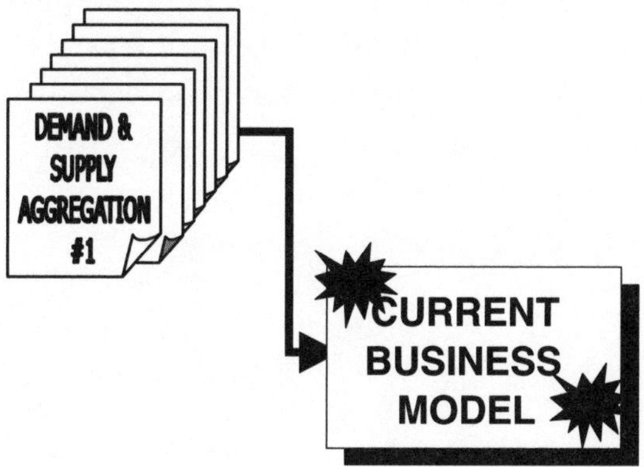

Once one has demystified the Internet and come to understand its 12 e-nablers, or capabilities, it becomes relatively easy to determine where the Internet will infringe on the current model. For example, if you are a company that uses large quantities of natural resources, it is easy to foresee that through the Internet, someone will set up a *market exchange* to bring buyers and sellers together to trade that resource at the best possible price. This new market exchange is bound to have an *impact* on how you purchase this raw material which is vital to your company. Thus, the concept of *points of impact.*

Step 3: Implications

To deal effectively with a problem, experts in the field of problem solving will tell you that one must understand the *implications* of that problem. In other words, it is almost impossible to deal with a situation whose cause or effects are not understood.

Therefore, once one has identified the points of impact the Internet will have on the current business model, the next step is to determine the *positive and negative implications* those points will have. Every point of impact will bring both types of implications. We do this for all the significant areas of impact.

An example is the situation mentioned above. The advent of an Internet *market exchange* is bound to have the following effects on that organization's purchasing function:

- On the negative side, it will bring more buyers into the bidding and may raise prices.
- On the positive side, the transaction costs may be reduced substantially.
- Once they are understood, these implications can be managed.

Step 4: Generating Internet Applications

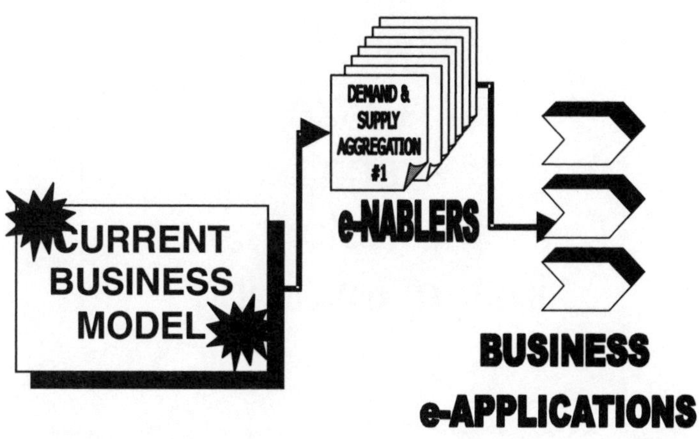

Once the implications of the points of impact are understood, it becomes relatively easy to think of ways in which the e-nablers can be applied to capitalize on using the Internet to the company's advantage.

For example, assume that we are involved in this process and represent the marketing function of the company. One activity of the marketing function is the generation of the monthly sales forecast. The current output is as follows:

* monthly sales estimates by product family

However, if we applied the *customer self-service* and the *build-to-order* e-nablers, we could produce the following output:

* daily sales by:
+ size
+ shape
+ color
* instant invoicing

The advantages of these new outputs in regard to our competitors are several:

More specific daily forecasts will allow us to reduce our raw materials inventory substantially.

Since the customer will tap directly into our system to specify and place the order, this eliminates the need for us to have a person do that, thus reducing our transaction costs.

More specific and daily orders will allow more frequent shipments to our customers.

Instant invoicing will accelerate customer payments and improve our cash flow and may give us a "float" period.

Our margins and profits will increase accordingly.

Manufacturing will be able to schedule production more accurately, thus reducing downtime.

Obviously, when we apply *all* 12 e-nablers to *all* the points of impact in our business model, we generate anywhere from 50 to

100 potential applications of the Internet to substantially improve our competitive position.

Step 5: Competitive Applications

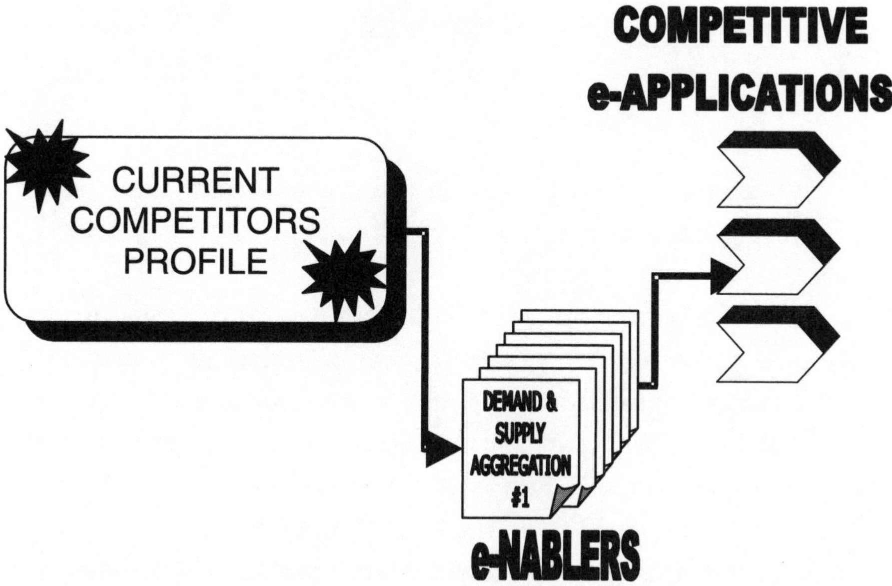

Another entity that will be the target of the Internet will be your competitors. Wouldn't it be interesting to know how your competitors will make use of the Internet? How can this occur? Very easily. By replicating their business model you can identify the Internet's points of impact and anticipate how each competitor will use the Internet to its advantage. You then "steal" the best applications you have generated and add them to your own. Your existing competitors, however, should not be your major concern in this new economy.

Looming in the shadows, there is a much more potentially dangerous new entrant, as shown in the graphic below.

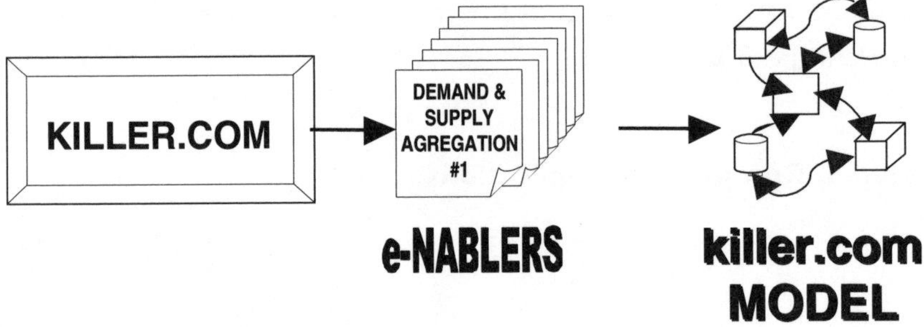

While you are concerned with your current competitors and how they will use the Internet, there is another entity being formed that should give you greater cause for concern.

Financed by millions of dollars from a venture capital firm, there is a new-economy entrepreneur that has developed an Internet-based business model whose sole purpose is to make yours obsolete, just as Amazon.com was designed to make obsolete the business models of Barnes & Noble and Borders and Priceline.com was designed to do the same to the airlines.

By using this process, however, one can anticipate what a killer.com model would look like and then set out to build that model *before* anyone else does. In other words, you neutralize the effect of a potential killer.com entry or cause a venture capital firm to think twice before investing in a start-up that would compete with an Internet-reinforced model.

In sessions with our clients who have used this process, this assignment is always the most revealing. We recommend that the team chosen to create the killer.com model consist of the company's youngest "techies." Management is always surprised by the "brutality" of such a model and also by the recognition that such a model is in fact viable. Their decision, then, is to create the killer.com or "steal" the best Internet applications that such a model would utilize and add them to the company's list.

Step 6: Choosing the Best Internet Applications

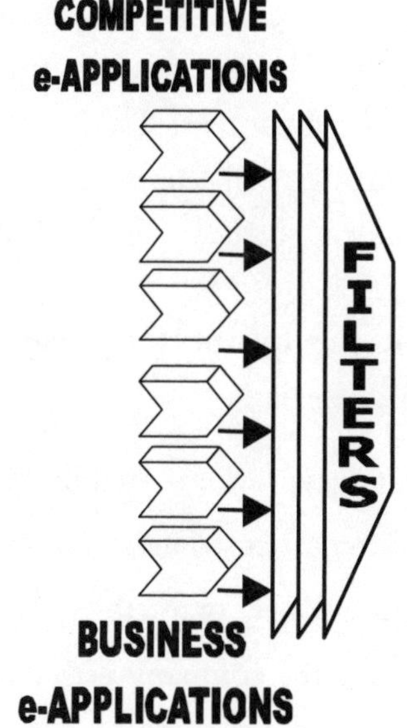

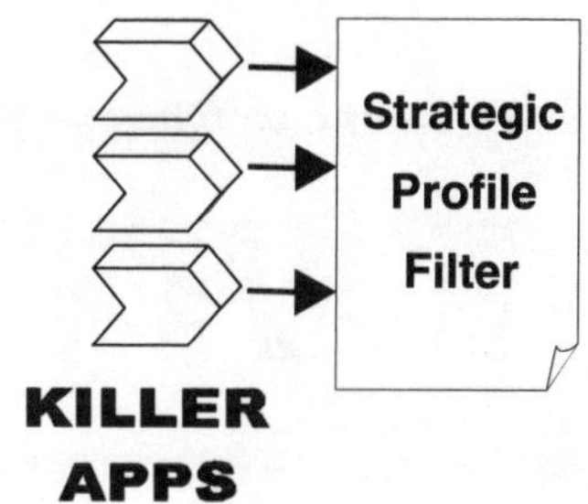

The previous steps in this process usually result in the creation of dozens of Internet applications that can be used to improve the business. The task, then, is to choose the best ones and base this choice on rational criteria. With this thought in mind, we now bring into this process two sets of filters.

The first filter is the *strategic filter*. One of the results of our strategic thinking process is the construction of a business concept which describes the underlying strategy of the enterprise. This concept then is converted into a binary filter which consists of six to eight questions that elicit a yes or no response. The more "no" answers the filter generates, the less good is the fit of the application to the strategy of the business. Thus, testing each Internet application against the strategy of the business will eliminate several of these concepts because they will be found not to fit this strategy.

Those which do fit the business strategy are then assessed against these additional criteria:

- Their ability to create new revenue streams
- Their ability to attract new customers
- Their ability to penetrate new markets
- Their ability to provide the company with a distinctive advantage
- Their ability to help the company change the rules of play

Step 7: Construct a Blueprint to Change the Rules of Play

If the first thing on your mind each morning is competitor A and the last thing on your mind each night is competitor B, that is a definite sign that you are obsessed with your competitors. This obsession derives from a "me-too" strategy that is not working. Winning companies are not obsessed with their competitors because they have a *distinctive* strategy that *sets them apart* from their competitors. Their way of dealing with their competitors is to look back over their shoulder periodically to ensure that the gap is getting wider.

Jeff Bezos, the CEO of Amazon.com, says it better than we could:

> Barnes & Noble and Borders are having trouble because it is hard to pursue me-too strategies on-line. In book retailing, Amazon.com still does the best job, and not by a little. The gap between us and our competitors is significant and grows every quarter.[1]

The goal of our strategic thinking process is to help a company develop a *business* strategy that will change the rules of play in its favor, and the same is true of our e-strategy process. The Internet applications that should end up on the blueprint are those which will enhance to the greatest degree a business strategy's ability to change the rules of play to the company's advantage.

[1]Forbes interview, June 2000.

The Nuts and Bolts of e-Strategy

Interview:
Heinrich Bossard, CEO,
Julius Brun,
Chief of Staff,
Bossard Group

Heinrich Bossard found himself in a position many CEOs have landed in lately. Investments in e-projects at the Swiss-based fastener supplier were growing rapidly, and even though Bossard's people were Internet-savvy for a bricks-and-mortar company, they lacked an agreed-upon strategy: Where do we want the Internet to take us? What are the most critical investments? Where are the most serious threats going to come from? What can we do about them? These are the kinds of questions that were keeping top management awake at night. Says CEO Heinrich Bossard,

> We had no Internet strategy. We had a lot of e-activities, not necessarily with just the Internet. We had customers and suppliers linked up. We had Electronic Data Input connections of all kinds, some order placement, and of course communications through e-mail. We were doing all kinds of things, but there was no strategy for it. We felt we were using too many resources with no focus. We needed to give it that focus.

Bossard had come to the realization that the company needed to develop a strategy not only in order to set technical priorities but also to detect threats to the business that the Internet might create, such as an e-competitor that could emerge and *make their business model obsolete.*

As Bossard puts it:

> We had taken the Internet seriously from the beginning. We had tried to stay ahead in technology. We knew the Internet could be an important part of our business, but we could also see that it was possible for someone to make us obsolete if they used the Internet in the proper way and we didn't. So it was in some ways a defensive wish to have an e-strategy to protect ourselves from becoming obsolete.

For a company such as Bossard, it is inevitable that the Internet will be more and more a cog in its business machine. With its head office in Switzerland and 60 offices worldwide, the company is a global supplier of "C-parts." C-parts are essential to the integrity of finished products, yet the parts themselves contribute little to the cost and value of a product. Bossard doesn't manufacture the parts; it is in effect a value-added reseller. Bossard's customers in many cases are multinational producers of everything from medical devices, to electronic instruments, to railcars.

As Bossard explains,

> In industry there are A-, B-, and C-parts. An A-part is the strategic part, which has a high value and a high impact on the product. Then there are B-parts, which have a lesser impact, and C-parts, which have even less. C-parts could be electronic components or tools or roller bearings or rubber elements or oil or whatever. Our specialty is fasteners. Actually, the C-parts are about 50 percent of the item which the industrial customer is buying. They take about 50 percent of the cost of purchasing and only about 5 percent of the value. This means the product itself, the C-part, cannot generate any competitiveness for the customer. Even if he gets it for free, it's a few percent

of the final product. And the process of having that many items and having them in stock all the time in the right qualities and the right standards is a hassle.

We had analyzed our business, and it came out generally that of the total cost of a fastening, the total *process* of fastening, only 15 percent is the hardware, like the washers, the nuts and the bolts. *Eighty-five percent is the process:* sourcing, purchasing, stocking, logistics, and the actual assembling technology. So if we can help a customer reduce this 85 percent of the cost, we can generate 40 to 70 percent savings on that and thus reduce the product cost by 10 to 20 percent. This sells more tractors, sells more scales, sells more machines. When we reduce the price on *the total cost* of a commodity item by 10 percent, it affects the competitiveness of the customer. That is why they outsource this whole process to us. Our goal, our focus, is helping our customers increase their competitiveness. This is our aim. And we can do that because fasteners are still the most used C-parts.

Bossard's services become an essential part of its customers' operations, a critical link in just-in-time manufacturing systems, removing the burden and lessening the cost of such noncore activities. To that end, Bossard has developed a sophisticated and unique process that goes from helping the customer select the right part for the product as it is being designed to managing inventory on the factory floor through innovations such as the SmartBin. SmartBin is a stocking bin equipped with a weight sensor which enables Bossard to monitor, through a computer, the precise level of inventory at any given time. This allows Bossard to connect the entire supply stream from the fastener producer to the production line. Obviously, the Internet can make this kind of process faster, cheaper and more effective, and Bossard was well into its efforts to realize the benefits the Internet might convey.

As most companies did, Bossard started with a home page and built piece by piece from there, quickly getting into much more exotic systems to support those services and deliver further value to the customer. Says this chief of staff, Julius Brun,

> The Bossard Group had a home page in 1996, redesigned in 1999. We also used the Internet for internal and external communication. In 1999 we had various projects using the Internet. We are in the process of building Boss Shop, a program to calculate the right fastener application, and Boss Calc, an application allowing the engineers to download CAD [computer-assisted drawing] of fasteners into their own CAD drawings. But we didn't have an e-strategy yet. These applications *were* built to support the overall business strategy, but we realized that we were starting to build various e-applications without a clear e-strategy. So we decided to build an e-strategy for the Bossard Group. We did an evaluation of different possible ways to do it, and the DPI e-strategy process was the most convincing.

Among the other approaches considered were those proposed by Internet solution providers, each with its own products and system to sell. Bossard's management preferred to use a method which would allow the company to examine the possibilities without the bias toward specific solutions that solution providers might be inclined to have.

Says Brun, "What attracted us was the process. They do not bring a solution; they bring you a process. This is *our* business, and *we* know how it works. That's why *we* are best suited to know how to get the answers. One of the companies we screened wanted to buy us plane tickets to Silicon Valley right away and show us this or that—totally solution-oriented. That's not what we wanted."

Adds Bossard, "Actually, DPI's methodology is process-oriented without distortion of the content. We weren't at that point looking for a particular solution. We were looking for a process to help *us* decide what we wanted the Internet to do for us. DPI's way gave us the opportunity to develop our own strategy by using their instruments *neutrally*, without bias toward a specific solution. They acted like a metronome. We had to play the piano, but they provided the metronome. They didn't try to impose any solutions. I always watched out for that during the process."

One of the obstacles most companies come up against in creating an e-strategy is that the people involved have widely disparate ideas about the Internet and its capabilities. This is quite natural in light of the newness of the technology. After all, for most business people the Internet has become a commercial reality only in the last three or four years. This syndrome makes it difficult to frame the discussion. There are no models to follow and no common language among the participants. Bossard's management group was no exception.

Comments Bossard,

> The understanding of the Internet among our managers was highly varied. We had a core of people who felt they were experts. And we still had people who believed it was a fad and would go away. We had people who thought, This is the last thing we should do now; let's wait until there's more experience in the market. Others felt, If we don't do it now, we'll be lost. Actual knowledge about the Internet, I would say, was generally higher in some than in others, and opinions as to what we should be doing varied all over the map.

The Bossard team found the e-nablers invaluable in cutting through the confusion, bringing a clarity that it lacked and badly needed. Says Bossard,

> The concept of the e-nablers did a lot of things. It really demystified the issues by navigating through the amorphous mass of e-

information. Before, we had a kind of a jumble developing. People were saying, "Have you heard of this, have you heard of that?" People went to seminars and were saying, "Why don't we do this or that?" "Everybody else is doing it. Why aren't we further along?" And the process helped us navigate through that amorphous mass and develop a proper understanding of what we want to do or don't want to do. It gave us the ability to position these e-nablers in our minds and have a common understanding of what we are talking about. We can label it and grasp what it is. This is a market exchange. This is a portal. Later on in the process this helped us understand which ones would help and not help us, but it was mainly mental to understand what are we talking about. Are we talking about a portal, or are we talking about a market exchange, or are we jumping from one into another? It gave us a common Internet language which the management now understands. So when we say we want to do this or this or this, we know what we're talking about.

Once an understanding of the e-nablers was established, Bossard's people were directed in the exercise of determining which e-nablers might have an impact on each of the core business processes. Then these impacts, plus or minus, were prioritized based on a filter created by the overall business strategy.

As Brun explains:

I think it was absolutely necessary to look at this map of our processes. It's a *must* to do that, because first of all, you have to have an understanding of what you do. So you have to map out the business processes. And when you do that, you have a common understanding of what you are doing on quite a high level. And then once you look at this and reflect and apply the e-nablers to it, all of a sudden you say, '*Aha*, that's where this one belongs. *Aha*, that's the way that works. *Aha*, that's how it could affect us. *Aha*, that's what we should do.

A picture of Bossard's Internet future began to take shape. The top people were able to see, from a strategic viewpoint, which of the various e-nablers would help or possibly damage them the most. It was possible to begin to generate a list of high- and low-priority e-initiatives, with a rationale for each rooted in the company's business strategy.

A LOOK AT E-COMPETITION

With an analysis of the internal processes nailed down, Bossard's people prepared to turn the company inside out. It was time to look at its business model from the perspective of competitors: known, existing competition *and* e-competitors that might emerge in the new Internet environment. The objective was to determine their areas of potential vulnerability or new opportunities where they might incorporate elements of new e-business models into their own model.

The next two steps in the process—*competitor.com* and *killer.com*—helped the company envision the future business "seascape" in order to develop a plan to deal with it.

Says Brun of the competitor.com segment of the process, "If you put yourself in the shoes of the competitor, you look at things from a different perspective. We found both competitor.com and killer.com very interesting, inspiring, and challenging. We gave killer.com special brilliance and asked 16 young professionals, none over age 30, to create the killer.com."

The object of that exercise was to flush out every CEOs worst nightmare: the upstart dot-com with $50 million in venture capital whose goal is to *put the company out of business.*

As Bossard recalls, "We brought together these 16 young people from all over the world. These are good ones, flexible, international ones. This was an excellent experience, on the one hand to see what these kids could do and on the other hand to find out where we were vulnerable and what opportunities we had."

Bossard explains the power of this step in the process:

> The benefit to creating the killer.com is to seriously work through a clear business plan for this new e-competitor that might appear and see how the company could work. We looked at several possible cases carefully, and some of these young guys really thought they could beat us. They were motivated. They were in a winning mood. One guy said to me when I came into the room, "You're a dead man walking." I was surprised, but I liked it. It meant they were committed to seeing the worst-case possibilities. The end result tells us what we need to anticipate and what elements we can incorporate now.

The debate about the possible impact of these potential e-competitors goes on, and the real future impacts cannot be defined with certainty, but forewarned is forearmed, as the saying goes.

Says the CEO,

> It showed us that some of those fantastic ideas cannot really hurt us too much. A killer.com might reach some segments which are not our core segments, but it could definitely not gain those segments which are our core segments. It shows where we have to be prepared for defense and where we don't have to, especially in areas where the total value of our services is not just product, where we have a richness of skills and capabilities that the customer requires and that would be very difficult to duplicate. We feel that the pure killer.com solutions, which are very, very much price-dominated, could not replace our engineering and logistics services because that's against the general tendency in the industry. People want technical services with the product. They can't fully replace those services, not the way we do it today. We are already much farther along than our

> competitors, and actually we often win in pitches because of our profound technological background and our logistics, even when we are more expensive. How would an auction or a price-oriented system deliver those services? This was the killer.com team's big headache. How could they overcome the very strong technical competence of Bossard? It takes up to two years for a customer to tie up with us fully to tap all the resources, and it's very hard to imagine that short-term auctioning would persuade our customers to risk all those achievements. But maybe I'll be wrong. We'll have to monitor it because we have the killer.com concept and will not forget it. We are using important elements of it. We have included it in our plan. Now we know what to look for. And if we see a killer.com company coming up, we will be very alert to certain issues. So thanks to this approach, we know how e-competitors will be likely to affect us.

Today Bossard Group has a comprehensive e-strategy that supports the company's business strategy. Because the Internet is evolving daily, the e-strategy will continue to be monitored and debated, evolving as new knowledge, technology, and ideas present themselves. Yet the Bossard team now has an agreed-upon basis of understanding from which to build.

States Bossard:

> For us, the e-strategy process was of tremendous importance. We were in a situation of destabilization because of the Internet. We felt insecurity and had conflicting solutions. We were at different stages of awareness, for instance, USA versus the rest of the world, or believers versus disbelievers. And all this has changed into a controlled management process with measurable results.
>
> Know what to do now. We have an e-strategy. We have always had a clear business strategy, and the fact that this process allowed us to be careful not to have the e-strategy take us away from our business strategy was very important. The management was deeply

involved, and so we have complete communication of the e-strategy. We are now able to say yes or no to new ideas, whether they're a fit or a nonfit, because we have an e-strategy. We know where we want to go. Before, it always made us nervous when something new came up. This has helped us arrange our resources better. So instead of tons of new and confusing ideas, we have an orderly approach. Our management now speaks one language, and so communications about new processes are better. I can see that it would have some major impacts such as a reduced risk of becoming obsolete and flexibility to tackle new opportunities. Our overall strategy is an excellent one at this stage. It really matches the needs of industrial OEMs [original equipment manufactures] in all major parts of the world, including China, America, and Europe. We really have services that go at the core of the current needs of the OEMs. E-enabling those processes isn't really generating more business yet, but we might become obsolete if we don't and somebody else does. So it's an offensive activity with a defensive character. For me this is strategically of the greatest importance: How can I protect my company from becoming obsolete in this new environment?

CHAPTER

Third Imperative: Integrating the Business Strategy and Internet Strategy Processes

As you probably have determined by now, our contention is that the Internet is another vehicle to help a company deploy its *business* strategy. Unfortunately, because of its pervasiveness, the Internet cannot be ignored. Because of the sums of money involved and the high level of risk, an astute CEO would want to begin by ensuring that those who are developing Internet applications clearly understand the business strategy of the enterprise.

THE ROLE OF THE CEO IN THE BUSINESS STRATEGY PROCESS

There is only one person in any organization who can drive the process of *strategic thinking*, and that is the chief executive of the organization. Pretending otherwise would be strategic foolishness. Strategic thinking must start at the top of any organization. This type of thinking is definitely a "trickle-down" process, not a "bubble-up" one. We usually recommend that the CEO include in the process all key "stakeholders" in the future of the business. This involves two groups of people: formulators of strategy and key implementers of strategy. In other words, it involves those who have something to contribute to the formulation of the strategy and those who can make or break its deployment.

It is a very interactive process, but the CEO must be the *owner* and show commitment to the process by participating in all the steps. Because it is highly interactive, this process is not for the faint of heart. It invites discussion, debate, and what we call "constructive provocation." During the process, everyone has the opportunity to express his or her views, have those views challenged, and then challenge the views of others. As a result, the process is ideal for CEOs who encourage frank, open discussion of the issues and challenges facing the business. CEOs who are not comfortable with this style of management should not use our process.

THE ROLE OF THE CEO IN THE e-STRATEGY PROCESS

Although over 60 percent of American companies have a Web site, only 25 percent sell anything on it. The reason for this seems to be the role that the CEO takes vis-à-vis the development of an e-strategy.

Our view on this topic is straightforward. The CEO must, as in setting the *business* strategy through the strategic thinking process, be the owner of the e-strategy process.

The Internet will change the genetic code of every organization and transform how companies conduct their business in the future. For this transformation to occur, the charge must be led by the CEO. Unfortunately, because of their lack of knowledge about the Internet, many CEOs have abdicated ownership to the Chief Information Officer or the Chief Technology Officer. There is only one person who can affect radical change in an organization, and that is the CEO.

One role that the CEO should not attempt to play is that of *process facilitator.* One cannot have one foot in the process and one foot in the content. Attempting to guide the process while participating in the debate gives everyone the impression that the CEO is trying to manipulate the process to a predetermined conclusion. Therefore, it is wise to have an outside third party guide the process along. The facilitator's role is to keep the process objective, honest, balanced, and moving from one set of conclusions to the next.

THE ROLE OF THE PROCESS FACILITATOR

First a few thoughts on the word *facilitator.* In our perspective, a facilitator, is not a *moderator.* A moderator is a person who directs traffic as well as he or she can during a meeting but without using any specific process. A process facilitator plays a very different role. This is a person who comes to the meeting with a structured process together with specific instruments that keep the discussion moving forward in a constructive manner. It is the duty of the facilitator to ensure that the participants have debated all the key concepts of the strategy—driving force, areas of excellence, and so on—and reached a consensus. The facilitator also keeps the process honest, balanced, and objective.

THE LOGISTICS OF THE STRATEGIC THINKING PROCESS

The strategic thinking process incorporates seven steps:

- Clarification of the current profile
- Analysis of the environmental variables
- Identification of the driving force options and development of possible strategic profiles and scenarios
- Choice of a tentative future strategic profile
- Development of competitive profiles
- Identification of critical Issues
- Final strategic profile

STRATEGIC THINKING PROCESS

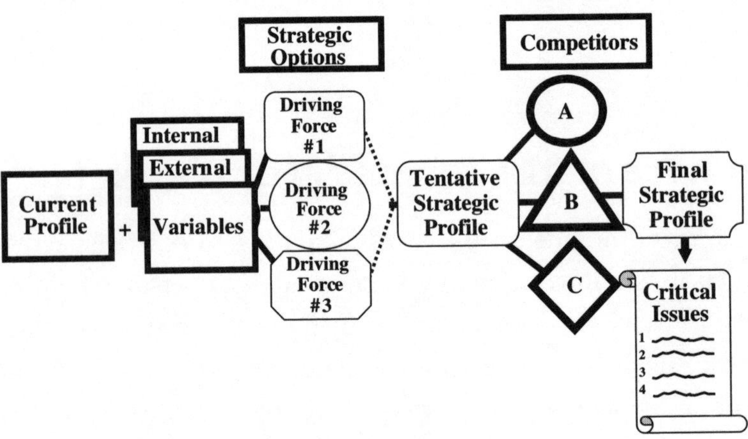

Clarification of the Current Profile

It is very difficult to have a discussion about what an organization should look like in the future without understanding what that organization looks like today. Therefore, the first step is to understand the common characteristics that cut through the current products, customers, market segments, and geographic markets. This allows one to understand the business's current driving force, current areas of excellence, and current strategy. This first step gives management a snapshot of the business in its current form. This is the start of strategic thinking.

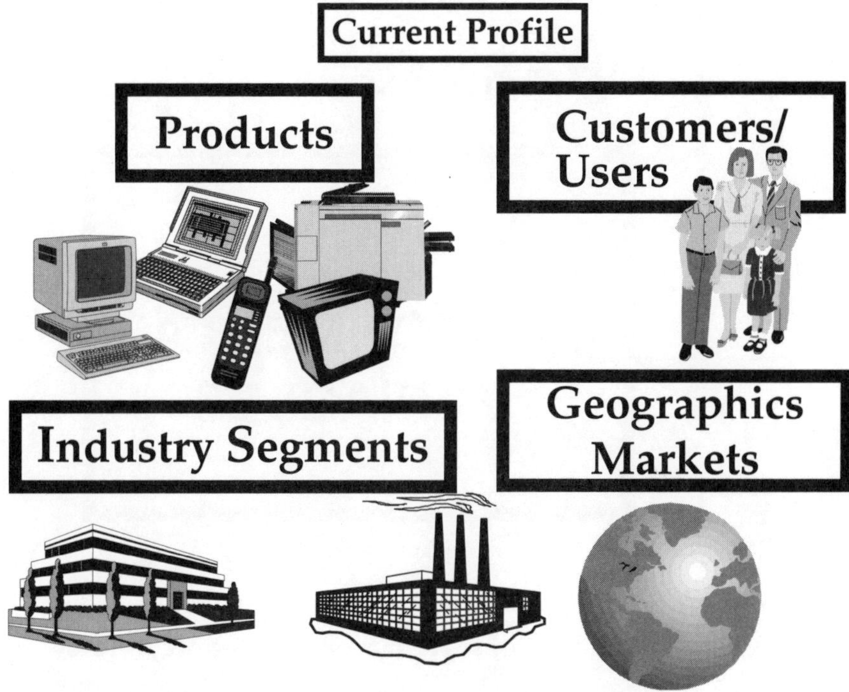

Analysis of the Environmental Variables

A strategy for the future of an organization should not be an extrapolation of the current strategy but instead must be constructed to accommodate the environment the company will face in the *future.* Since that environment could be very different from the environment it encountered in the past, the second step is an analysis of these variables.

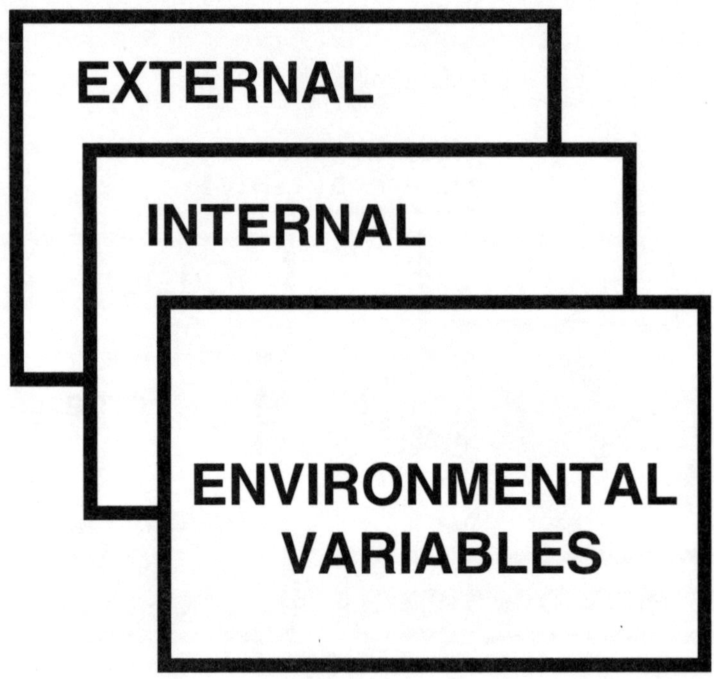

These variables are usually highly subjective in nature and represent each person's view of what may or may not occur inside—and, more important, outside—the organization. These differing views must be discussed in a rational manner so that everyone involved can agree on the most important factors the business will have to face in the future. At DPI, we discuss all the variables each person sees and get agreement on the "significant few."

The quality of the strategic inputs determines to a great extent the quality of the output from the process. Since the best inputs are stored in the heads of the key people who run the company, we have designed a Strategic Input Survey that seeks responses from each member of the management team in 11 key facets of the internal and external environment. These responses are obtained before the work session, are edited and collated by us, and become the "raw material" for this session.

Development of Strategic Scenarios Stemming from Different Driving Forces

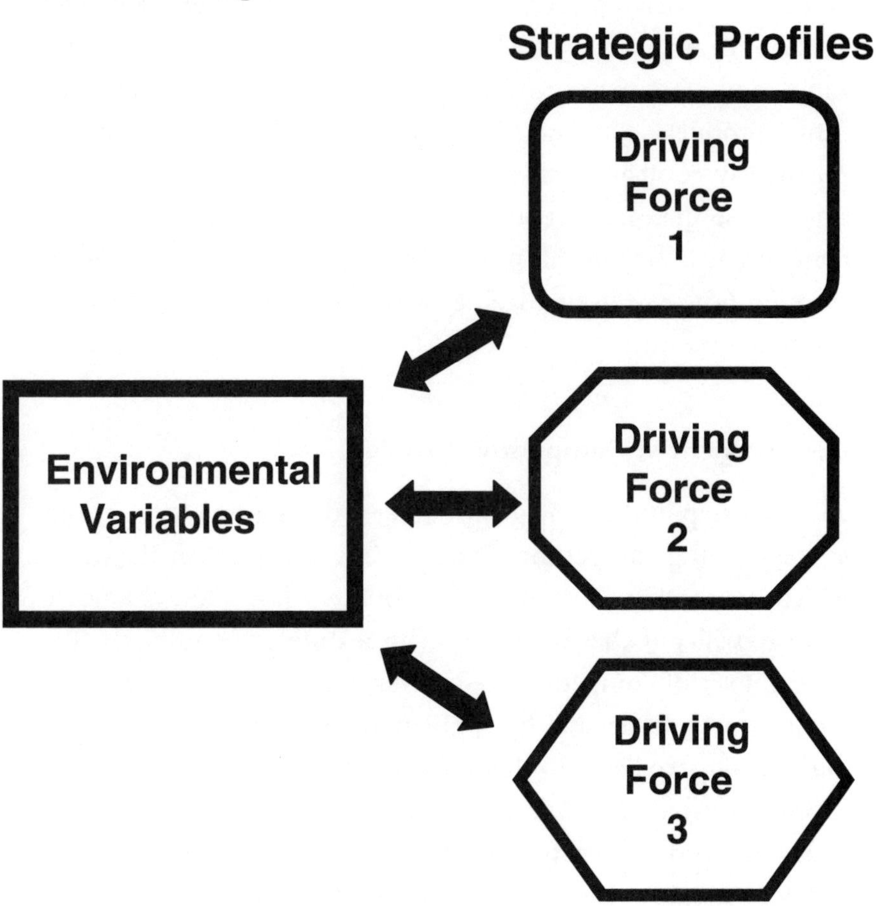

Once the management team has agreed on the variables that will work for or against the organization in the future, it can explore which one, two, or three components of the business could be the "engine," or *driving force*, of its future strategy. No company can just change from one driving force to another, but many companies have two or three capabilities that could be the engine for a future strategy.

We bring a methodology to help management understand these two or three areas which represent their strategic options and possible driving force of their strategy. We then have management draw profiles of where each one would lead the organization and what the organization would look like in terms of the future products, customers, and markets it would and would not pursue. By comparing these profiles to each other, management can choose the one best suited to deal with the environment the company will face in the future. Management has now chosen a *tentative future strategy*, together with a *strategic profile* of what it wants to become.

Development of Competitive Profiles

The next step in the strategic thinking process is an analysis of the strategy of the competitors the company will meet in the *future*, which may not be the ones it encounters now. Any change of strategy will put the organization in a different sandbox with a different set of competitors. However, we can identify who these competitors will be and, by applying the concepts of *driving force and areas of excellence* to them, anticipate their strategy and draw profiles of what each one will emphasize more and less in terms of future products, customers, and markets. By doing this, management can also take action to manage their strategy and change the rules of play to the company's advantage.

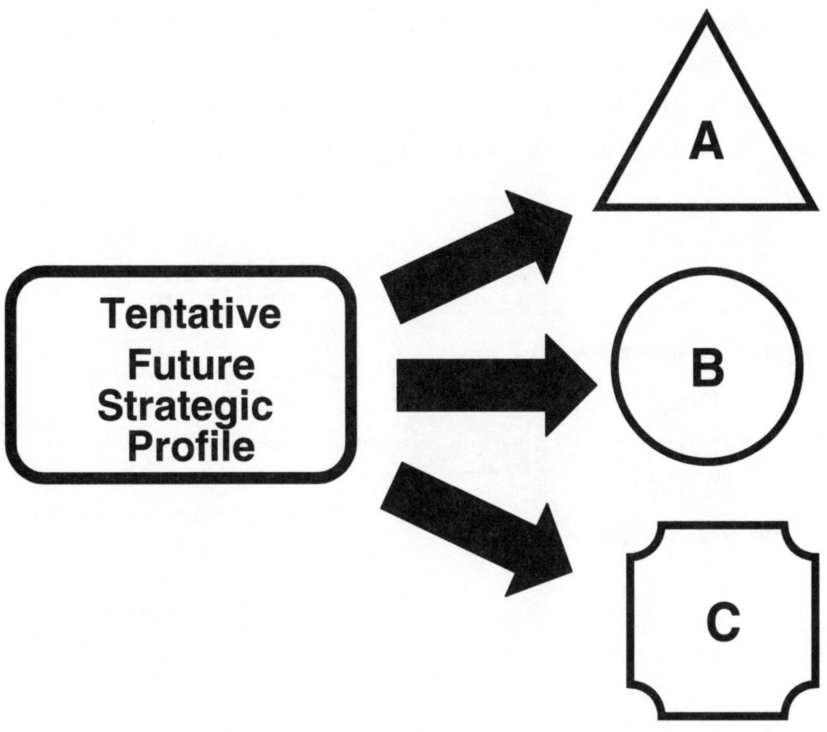

Identification of Critical Issues

When CEOs change the strategy and direction of an organization, they often do not think through the *implications* of that change. As a result, they end up reacting to these implications as they "bump" into them. Every change in strategy—even a minor one—will bring implications of one kind or another. If management wants its new strategy to succeed, it must now devote some time to thinking through the implications of the strategy and identifying the *critical issues* that stand in its way.

These critical issues become the *agenda* for management. Each issue is assigned an *owner* who will be held accountable for getting the issue resolved; action steps are identified, and completion dates are agreed to. It is the resolution of these critical issues that assures the successful deployment of the strategy.

One of the issues that surfaces in every strategy project is the need to develop an Internet strategy, which is the process we explore next.

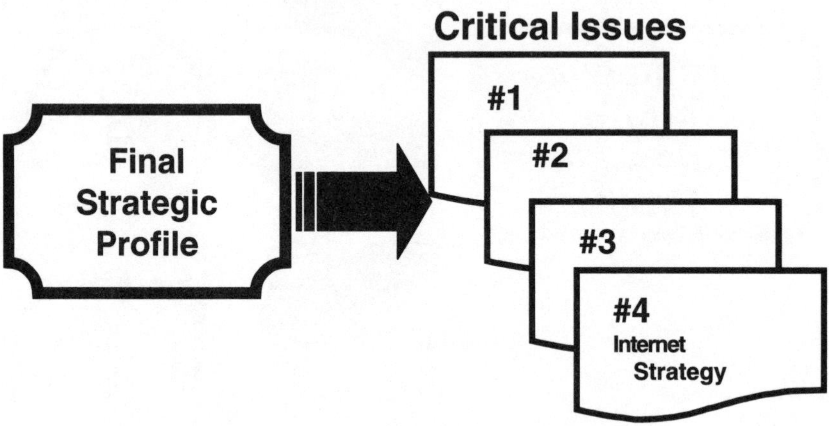

INTEGRATING THE TWO PROCESSES

As we mentioned in a previous chapter, the Internet has surfaced as a critical issue at the end of every strategic thinking project we have been involved in in the last three years. In other words, the Internet is on every CEO's radar screen. However, because of the e-nigma phenomenon, most companies are addressing this issue in a fragmented manner. Several functions, independently of each other, are experimenting in one way or another. In principle, experimentation is good, but piecemeal experimentation without an overall corporate blueprint can result in costly, incompatible systems that may not support the strategic direction of the business.

As we did in the business strategy area, we have been able to open the black box and *codify* the process of formulating and deploying an Internet strategy that supports the business strategy of the enterprise. The process has six phases over a six- to nine-month time frame. The following graphic illustrates this process of integration.

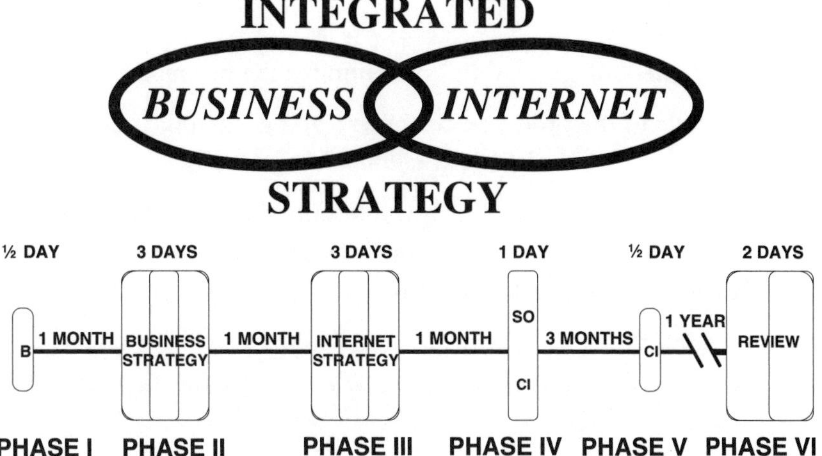

Phase I: Briefing Session

This session is intended to accomplish the following outcomes:

- Give the selected members of the strategy formulation team (SFT) an understanding of the overall scope of the 12-month project.
- Introduce the SFT to the concepts and process of strategic thinking.
- Introduce the SFT to the Strategic Input Survey and coach the members on how to respond to the questions that relate to the internal and external variables the organization will encounter in the future.

Phase II: Strategic Thinking Work Session

Approximately one month later there is a three-day session of the SFT which is facilitated by a DPI professional and delivers the following outcomes, using the strategic thinking process described in the last chapter:

A clear statement of strategy and direction for the business

A clear profile of the products, customers, and geographic markets the company will pursue and those it *will not*

A short list of critical issues which will become management's work plan and whose resolution will take the organization from where it is today to what it wants to be in the future.

Introduction of the e-strategy team (EST) to the prework document and coaching the team members on how to prepare for the next session

Phase III: e-Strategy Session

This three-day session is dedicated to the use of our e-strategy process. It delivers the following outcomes:

An Internet strategy that is integrated and supports the business strategy of the company

A *blueprint* of prioritized Internet applications by mode of Net

A list *of business requirements separated into musts and wants* for each application

Phase IV: Strategic Objectives

One month later, there is a one-day work session which has two outcomes:

The development of *offensive* positions that the company must capture to make its strategy succeed

The development of *defensive* positions that the company must defend at all costs to make its strategy succeed

Phase V: Monitoring Progress

During the next six months, there are two quarterly one-day meetings with the CEO and the "inner circle." These meetings have the following outcomes:

A review of the status of each *strategic* critical issue on management's list

A review of the status of each Internet application project

Phase VI: Review

This session is a review or revisit of our previous conclusions twelve to fourteen months prior, which allows management to fine-tune and tighten the company's strategic focus.

MAKING THINKING A REPEATABLE BUSINESS PRACTICE

> Thinking is a difficult activity . . . which is why most people never do any of it.
>
> Henry Ford

One of our client's calls us a strategic enforcer. "If we hadn't scheduled this meeting with you, we would find a reason not to have it." He goes on, "But since you're going to be here, we show up.

And we know what questions you're going to ask, so we work our butts off to get things done because none of us want to go into that room and report: 'no progress.' "

This is a fair assessment of our role with the CEO and the management team. We "obligate" them to use structure and discipline to address issues which most executives do not have the willpower to impose on themselves. However, good processes do it pain-free and in a time-efficient manner, which is what our processes do.

In fact, most of our clients will repeat these processes in divisions, business units, and subsidiaries. These concepts grow on executives, and as they achieve better and better results, over time the concepts are utilized over and over to the point where they become the modus operandi of the enterprise.

Integrating Strategy and e-Strategy

Interview:
Neil McDonough,
President, FLEXcon

Critical thinking processes are second nature to the people at FLEXcon. From developing the corporate strategy to solving problems on the production line, decision-making teams have used DPI's processes for the last decade. When the Internet became a critical issue, DPI's e-strategy process presented the means to sort it out, determine how it fit the company's business strategy, and proceed with a coherent corporate plan the company would be comfortable with.

FLEXcon is a privately held maker of laminated adhesive-backed materials that are used in diverse applications from labels for shampoo and wine bottles to membranes for touch pads and holographic security indicia. Since reaching the $100 million mark in the mid-1980s, the company has seen its growth accelerate, targeting $400 million in 2000. Part of that success can be attributed to a strategic clarity that pervades the company, a direct result of going through the strategic thinking process and revisiting the strategy every three years as a reality check.

The president and the managers at FLEXcon have found that this common strategic understanding has formed the basis for all future decisions, including sorting out unexpected challenges such as the Internet.

Says FLEXcon's president, Neil McDonough:

> It all comes down to getting agreement on the driving force and the business concept and developing the critical issues from there. It's very straightforward. You've just got to invest the time and do it and do it with a facilitator who has the experience to force you through these questions and keep the process on track. Then, once you've gotten down to the critical issues, you give people the tools to make the right decisions and get things done. If you're going to tackle complex issues, you've got to embed these concepts in your company's culture.

As it has at most companies over the last few years, the Internet has grown in strategic importance for FLEXcon. As it has evolved into new ways to communicate with customers, suppliers, and employees, the Internet has required more and larger investments, and so has come to require an overall plan that passes a company's "strategic filter."

Like most companies, FLEXcon had developed a Web site to provide basic information about the company to anyone who wanted to know. Says McDonough, "We had our Web site, which was essentially a printed electronic brochure. We had the ability to receive e-mail. We had in fact received an order or two, which surprised us. But it was basically general information, not even very specific product information. We had our future plans to include data sheets and a product selector and other things we were working on, but what we actually were doing was just a visual Web site."

As the capabilities of the Internet and its users developed, a steady stream of ideas began to come forward, each with a rationale to back it up. McDonough says:

> It was pieces of things. It was driven by whoever was the most vocal and thought we ought to have this or that. I wasn't feeling bad about

it in the sense that the arguments were persuasive and driven from our strategy and all the things that we were talking about doing to grow the business. But it was not a whole, coordinated, cohesive plan: what should go first, what should go second, and so on.

I saw it as *linked* to the strategy but not *integrated.* It certainly wasn't a situation where people were saying we ought to create a whole different e-business division. It wasn't anything like that, but neither was it integrated into every aspect of our strategy, what really fit and would make the most sense as a whole. The discussions went on. Do we really want to have data sheets out there, or don't we want to talk to people directly? There was always a back-and-forth going on. And of course, all the offers were coming in from the "portals," the aggregator guys who want to represent the industry and do auction sites or be the connection point. So, do we join one of these and pay that fee or not join one of these, maintain our own direct contact, but lose out on those chances? So that was a constant battle.

The company's management needed to develop the same kind of common strategic confidence in its growing Internet investments that it had in other major capital investments. Therefore, when DPI developed its e-strategy process, FLEXcon jumped on the opportunity:

I had a goal going into this process, and it was a very simple one: to have a comfort level with what we were doing and the pace we were doing it at. We liked the fact that *we* could make this evaluation and it wasn't just a techie coming in and talking about what *could* be. It was more an approach of what *should* be, based on who we are and how we see the world.

One of the concepts that caught McDonough's attention was the twelve e-nablers which help translate the various capabilities of the Internet into tangible business terms. Tentatively plugged into various business and information processes within the company, they form a test bed for evaluating various ideas. McDonough says:

> I thought that was a great way of presenting what the Web could do. One by one, you're essentially trying these capabilities on like a suit of clothes. And you say, "How does this fit, how does this feel?" And most of them you reject because you say, "That's not our business." You get a much better understanding of what they are. The popular press will tell you how Amazon operates or how the auto suppliers are going to aggregate and put out for bids through an aggregate site, that sort of thing. But the e-nablers let us look at all those different models more closely and see how they might apply to our business specifically. So it was a good way to be able to try on the different business models that you're not familiar with because they weren't part of the world ten years ago.

Another aspect of the e-strategy process McDonough found essential was the competitive analysis portion. He and his management team are old hands at analyzing their competitors' strategies to be able to anticipate their future behavior, having done it extensively in their strategic thinking sessions. McDonough saw the competitor.com and killer.com segments of the process as compelling from both offensive and defensive strategic standpoints. This exploration of the competitive aspects of the Internet allowed the company to evaluate how its competitors might be able to use the Internet to take business away from it. By looking at FLEXcon as an e-competitor might, they have begun to see how they may be able to tip the balance in any future playing field to their own advantage—to change the rules of play to their favor.

As McDonough sees it,

> It's one thing when you're trying on the twelve models for how they fit you. There you're talking about what are your strengths, or areas

of excellence, that you're trying to work on. Here you're looking more into weaknesses, saying, "If I were on the outside, how could I attack FLEXcon and be successful?" And you try on some of those, and in some areas you feel pretty good because they could try that all they want, but they're not going to make much headway. And then you try on some others, and you say, "You know, it may only be a small part of my business, but that could make a competitor very healthy if they attacked and attacked in this way; they definitely could be successful for that part of the business." As you do that, you understand your vulnerabilities better and know what you need to do. It's kind of like Mike Robert's idea that attacking a competitor's weakness will only make that competitor stronger in the long run. When you see that, you start working on those weakness areas, and it actually helps you become a better company overall. But then the flip side of that is that if that's where you can be attacked, how could you use a similar strategy on some of your competitors? That's also very powerful. You're able to look at them, put yet another skin on yourself, and say, "If I did operate this way, I could get a part of *their* business."

This works very well, particularly because with the clearly delineated twelve e-nabler models you have something concrete to play with. It's not pie in the sky or theory as long as you can get out of your own skin long enough to really think, "If I had to start all over again and compete against my company, which one of these could I make the most headway with?" If you can get yourself thinking like that, you can see the effects of the Internet very clearly and make yourself stronger.

As it is to the majority of existing companies, to FLEXcon, the Internet is a set of tools to be used selectively to implement an ongoing strategy. The Internet will not affect every company in a particular business in the same way, since each player in that market has its own driving force, areas of excellence, and way of relating to its customers. Nor will the Internet affect every part of each business. It will effect, to greater and lesser degrees, individual parts of the value chain. Moreover, each company is a body in motion, with a business model that has worked to some degree. For the majority of companies, there is no need to toss out the existing model and start from scratch to build an e-model.

Says McDonough:

> The "why not" is that so much of our business is based on ongoing business relationships. The Internet is great for an exchange of information, but it doesn't match face-to-face, knee-to-knee contact with the customer. If you were able to do all your business over the telephone or over a fax, the answer would be: Yes, it absolutely could be at least partially replaced by the Internet. But I'm flying out at noontime today [Monday], and I'll be back on Thursday. I need that face-to face time with customers. And more importantly, my technical people need that face-to-face time with suppliers and customers. So I see the Web as *another* tool but not a *replacement* tool. Could it replace the fax machine just as the fax replaced the telex? Sure. But it isn't replacing our business model.

The e-strategy process gives companies a framework to examine carefully each piece of the information stream from raw material to customer and identify where each e-nabler may add value or pose a threat. The relative value or threat then can be examined through the lens of the strategy. Based on that prioritization, individual applications can be designed and implemented to satisfy the most pressing needs of the business. As McDonough explains it:

> This e-strategy process has changed the way we're prioritizing what we're doing with the Internet. For us it mostly has to do with how

we work with present customers and reach new customers. We believe we're doing a good job with our current customers, and the Internet can improve but not radically change that. The big driver for FLEXcon is reaching new users we haven't been in contact with before. It will be just one method to do that, but a very important one, we believe.

What's the Net Result for FLEXcon?

As McDonough explains it:

> It's the comfort level of the whole team, the fact that we've got an e-strategy. It's not the most aggressive strategy in terms of the use of the Web, but it's the most appropriate strategy in terms of the use of the Web for who we are, who the customers are, and what we're trying to accomplish. We're comfortable that we're not either falling behind or trying to do the wrong thing first but are in fact choosing very appropriately which things to do and which not.
>
> But that comfort level is going to last only a short time, because with the Internet, things will change. We'll have to do a check again, much faster than we do our every-three-years strategy check. I think I'd like to go through the e-strategy process at least once more, if not twice more. One, because of the refinements that DPI's going to make as they do it multiple times, and two, because it takes a while before you really grasp it all. The second time through I'm sure I will hear things that I didn't understand or hear the first time. So much of adult learning is learning it when you need to know it. Also, the Internet is constantly changing, so we'll have to keep looking at it in the future.

McDonough also believes that if the e-strategy is integrated with the business strategy, its creation and re-creation will give

FLEXcon another opportunity to refine its overall strategic approach.

As McDonough explains,

> I thought the process itself was a great strategy review tool, because we have to go back to the fundamentals of our strategy again before we say, "How does the business potentially apply to this area or that area in the Internet?" So it may actually serve as a great three-year check on our strategy in addition to what's going on with us and our competitors and our areas of expertise. If you think the Internet is going to affect your strategy in some way, it will come out in this.
>
> As it came out in the end, the e-strategy is just a part of our overall strategy and business concept. And it's using the Web where it's best used, to support the initiatives we already had going on in terms of end-user contact, more information to customers, data sheets, and the drive to make a product configurator that we're going to use for our telesales people. This configurator would also be capable of being put on the Web and used by end users to make product selections based on their needs.
>
> What the e-strategy process did was allow us to have a framework that allows us to dovetail applications together so that we don't make essentially a print brochure and then have to do everything for an electronic brochure. We now have the internal rules to standardize the thought that what we're putting on the Web, we need to be able to do in print. What we need to do in print, we need to be able to put on the Web. And then not constantly reinvent. We have our options prioritized, and my comfort level is much higher now. These can be major investments, and I need to be sure we're doing the things that best support our strategy.

CHAPTER

The Tangible and Intangible Results

Our research on the development of an e-strategy process began in earnest in 1998 and culminated in mid-2000. During that period we worked with some two dozen of our clients in a beta mode. As the process took shape, we offered it to other clients, and another two dozen or so have also employed it. We chose clients that represented a broad spectrum of industries, small, medium, and large in size and based in five countries, some international in scope and others only domestic.

Approximately six months after their use of the e-strategy process, we asked each CEO to tell us what results, if any, he or she had seen. Their answers were remarkably similar and fell into two categories: *tangible* and *intangible.*

TANGIBLE RESULTS

The tangible results were the ones the process was designed to produce. The process was designed to generate the following "hard" outputs.

Coherent Corporate Blueprint

The first output the process delivers is a corporatewide coherent blueprint of multiphased Internet applications that stem from an analysis of the Internet's impact on a company's business model, on its competitors' business models, and on the model of a potential killer.com model.

These applications are also classified by the form of Net they are best suited for, such as Intranet, Extranet, or Internet. Also generated are the *business requirements* each application must meet. These are the requirements that can be given to an IT solution provider after which they are used to create *technical specs* from which a request for proposal can be produced. This process is shown in the following two graphics.

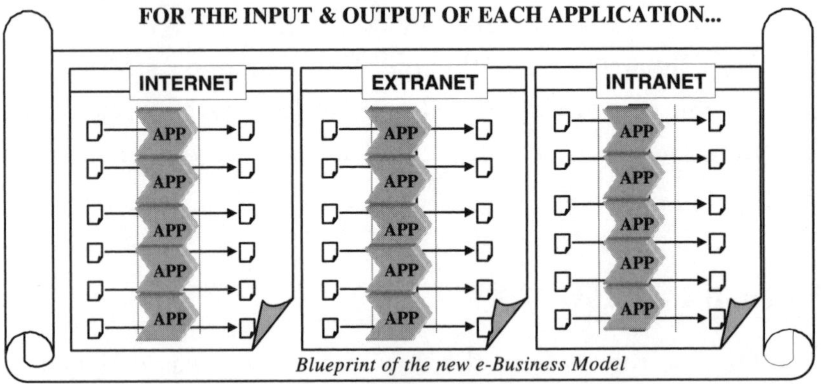

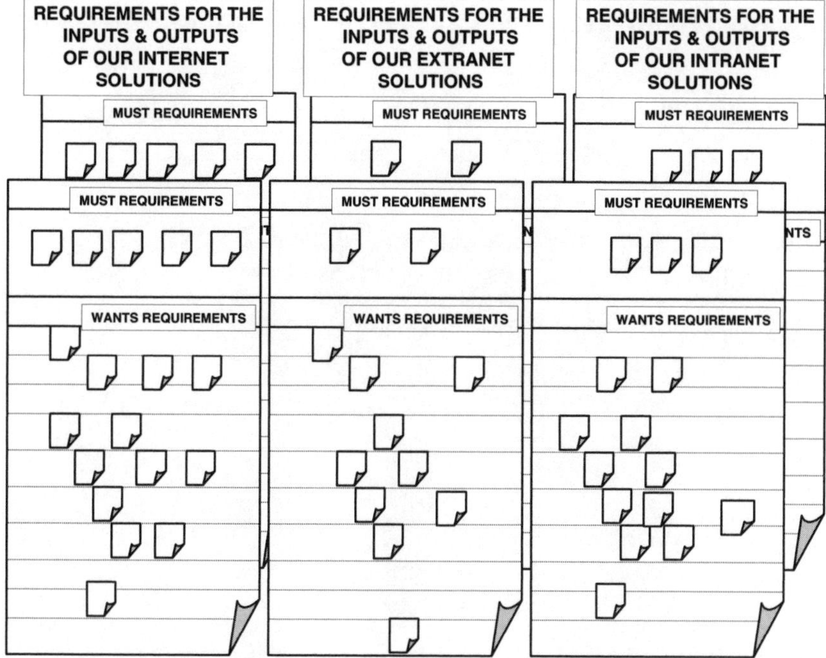

Prioritized Applications

A second tangible outcome of the process is a short list of the Internet applications that will have the most significant impact on the following areas of the business:

- The ability to create new revenue streams for the company
- The ability to acquire new customers
- The ability to open new market segments or geographic areas
- The ability to provide the company with a distinctive and sustainable competitive advantage
- The ability to change the rules of play to the company's advantage

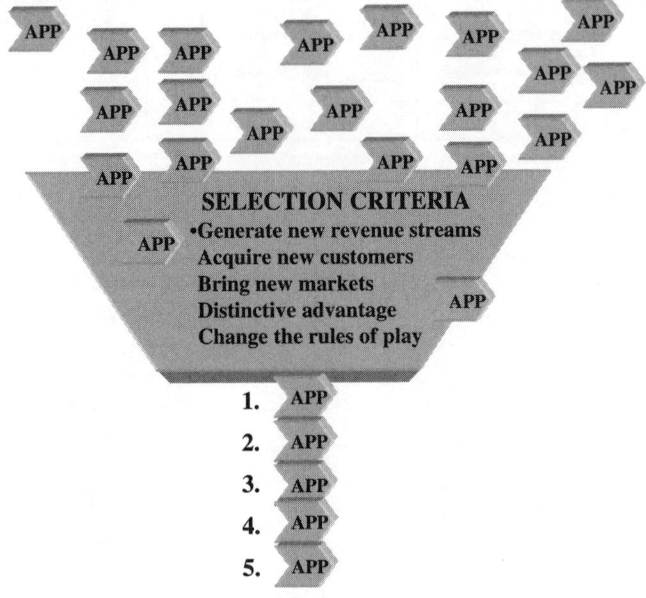

Integrated Business and Internet Strategies

Another result of this process is an integrated business and Internet strategy which eliminates the Catch-22 syndrome in which the client blames the IT consultant and the consultant blames the client for the failure of a project.

We have been told by IT consultants who participated in sessions with our clients that if every client would articulate his or her requirements as well as our process does, the proposals submitted would be more on target and the solutions would be implemented more quickly, cost much less money, and have a substantially higher probability of success. In fact, one consultant even admitted that they all include a "fudge" factor equal to 15 percent of the total proposal cost to cover the time spent attempting to identify the client's requirements.

VISION
DIRECTION
STRATEGY
INTRANET
EXTRANET
INTERNET
STRUCTURE
SKILLS
COMPENSATION

Insurance Policy

The overall result of using the process in a company is that it is an insurance policy against the high failure rate of IT projects. By being the architect of your own e-strategy, you reduce the probability of failure by increasing the probability of your own people generating Internet applications that result in new business processes that give your organization a *distinct competitive advantage.*

"Insurance Policy" Against the High Failure Rate of IT Projects

INTANGIBLE RESULTS

When we held debriefing sessions with the CEOs who were early users of our process, they also commented on another by-product they had not counted on. These were "soft," or more intangible, in nature, but the CEOs seemed to place almost as much value on these outputs as they did on the tangible ones.

INTANGIBLE RESULTS

- Client = Architect Ø Consultant
- In-House, Shared Ownership
- More Effective Deployment
- Demystifies The Internet
- Repeatable Business Practice

Demystification of the Internet

One after another, every CEO thus far has told us that our explanation of the enablers took the mystery out of the Internet and made it understandable. As a result, some told us, they could conjure ways to apply the Internet to some areas of their businesses and widen the distance between themselves and their competitors.

Control of One's Destiny

Because we included key managers and senior executives of the client's organization in our process, several CEOs felt in control of their destiny since they were the "architects" of their own e-strategies, as opposed to being at the mercy of an outside IT consultant. Using an outside consultant to develop an e-strategy is akin to outsourcing your *thinking*, whereas involving your own people is tantamount to *insourcing* your *thinking*.

More Rapid Deployment

The "speed" gurus will tell you that doing things faster than your competitors can is a critical factor for success. If you think that you have an e-strategy but are not deploying it fast enough, the speed gurus will then tell you that you need to invest millions of dollars to "automate" your Internet-based and non-Internet-based IT systems.

Our view is different. We feel that if you think that automating your business processes will accelerate the deployment of the business strategy or the Internet strategy, you are in for an unpleasant surprise. It is difficult to determine *how* to improve something when you do not know *what* it is that you want to do.

Our experience has shown us that most people in a company do *things right*. Unfortunately, they are frequently blamed for doing *things wrong*. In other words, they are doing *things right* but doing the *wrong things*. Our e-strategy gets your people to identify the *right things* to work on so that people who do *things right* are working on the *right things*. Once agreement is reached about *what* to do, the debates stop and the people concentrate on deployment. Several CEOs have told us how surprised they were to see things start happening much more quickly than before and said that the DPI process was the major catalyst for that phenomenon.

Repeatable Business Practice

What's the first thing a chemist does after having successfully completed an experiment using different chemicals? She immediately writes down the formula she used.

Why does she do this? The answer is simple. First, so that she can repeat the experiment a second time and get the same result. Second, so that she can transfer this newly found knowledge to other employees of the firm. The message is: Anything that cannot be codified is extremely difficult to transfer to others.

In business, anything that cannot be codified cannot be turned into a *repeatable business practice.* However, once the process has been experienced and seen in "hard-copy" form, it becomes relatively easy to institutionalize the process and turn it into a repeatable business practice that can be used over and over.

Index